TAKEDOWN

Books by Matt Christopher

TAKEDOWN

Matt Christopher

Illustrated by
Margaret Sanfilippo

LITTLE, BROWN AND COMPANY
Boston   Toronto   London

FIRST EDITION

The characters and events in this book are fictitious. Any
similarity to real persons, living or dead, is coincidental and not
intended by the author.

Library of Congress Cataloging-in-Publication Data
Christopher, Matt.
  Takedown / Matt Christopher; illustrated by Margaret
Sanfilippo.
    p.   cm.
  Summary: As he is helped by an assistant referee to prepare
for a wrestling match with the neighborhood bully, Sean begins
to wonder if his mentor could be his long-lost father.
  ISBN 0-316-13930-0
  [1. Wrestling — Fiction.] I. Sanfilippo, Margaret, ill.
II. Title.
PZ7.C458Tad 1990
[Fic] — dc19
                                                      89-31645
                                                        CIP
                                                         AC

10 9 8 7 6 5 4 3

MV
Published simultaneously in Canada
by Little, Brown & Company (Canada) Limited

PRINTED IN THE UNITED STATES OF AMERICA

To Richard and Celeste

A special thanks to my nephew, Craig Christopher, former wrestler at Lansing Central School, Lansing, New York, and to Coach Jim Barnes, wrestling coach at Rock Hill High School, Rock Hill, South Carolina, for their help with the wrestling portions of this book.

TAKEDOWN

1

One minute the street in front of us was completely empty. The next minute three guys appeared as if by magic. Each was about my age, but bigger — about the size of my stepbrother, Carl. They stood spread-legged in the middle of the street, glaring at us as if to say, "Come on! If you've got the guts!"

"Look!" Carl cried, his voice frightened. "It's that new kid they call the Octopus! And two of his punk buddies!"

I recognized them, too. Max Rundel, "the Octopus," was in the middle. Hunter Nyles, "the Squasher," was on his right, and John McNeer — who hadn't earned a crazy nickname, yet — was on his left. Rundel had moved

3

into Mount Villa during the summer and already had created a name for himself. And I don't mean just the nickname pinned on him because of his wrestling style. He had also gained a reputation as a leader, and if you refused to follow him you'd pay for it, one way or another. Anyway, that's the word that got around.

Me, I'm no follower, and I don't intend to be.

"Go past 'em!" I yelled at Carl, who was riding his dirt bike on my right side. "You swing to the right, I'll swing to the left!"

I don't often order Carl around. Even though I'm two years older, he's bigger than I am. It's generally he who tries to give me orders. But I seldom, if ever, pay attention to them.

This time he didn't say anything, and I didn't look to see what kind of expression he had on his face, either. I had no time.

I wheeled to the left and Carl wheeled to the right. At the same time the guys split up, Nyles sweeping directly into my path. A scared look came over his suntanned face, as if he thought I was going to smash right into him.

But I took my thumb off the gas lever and braked, stopping less than a yard in front of him, and looked him straight in the eye. Then I glanced at Carl and saw that he'd done the same thing with McNeer.

"What d'you think you're doing?" I snapped at Nyles. "Who says you own the street?"

"I says," Max answered, sounding like a tough army sergeant.

I stared at him. He was about five-ten, with heavy eyebrows and wavy blond hair that swept back over his head and ended in a bunch of curls behind his neck. His cream-colored shirt and frosted blue jeans were so tight I wondered how he'd gotten into them. A round button with I AM KING inscribed on it was pinned to his shirt.

"Off," Nyles said, grabbing the handlebars of my bike. "Off! You hear me?"

I glared at him, my heart thumping like a hammer, then glanced back at Max. He grinned at me, one of those grins you'd like to

wipe off with a fist. "You heard him, Bailor. Off! We'd like to check out your wheels. Nothing wrong in that, is there?"

"There sure is!" I yelled, and socked Nyles's hand with a fist. "Out of my way, Nyles!" I shouted, and started to twist the gas lever.

"Oh, no, you don't!" Max yelled as he rushed at me, grabbed my leg, and started to pull me off my bike. "Off, Bailor!" he snarled again. "This is no joke, Squirt!"

I couldn't believe this! What guts! Did he think they could take our bikes from under us without our putting up a fight? I didn't know about Carl, but *I* wasn't going to let them get away with it!

I shut off the engine as Max dragged me off the seat, and, moving as fast as I could, I grabbed him around both legs. He went down like a sack of potatoes. I landed on top of him, got my right leg around his thighs in a scissors hold and started to wrap one arm around his neck. I was hoping to tie him up in a hold and make him promise to leave us alone, but I didn't count on him turning into a maniac. I guess I'd forgotten for a minute that this was no wrestling match but a street fight, and that Max Rundel would use any method he could to win.

He squirmed out of my hold in nothing flat, slugged me on the jaw, then sat on my back with one hand pressed against my head and the other bending my left arm up between my shoulder blades.

"Wrestler, too, huh, Bailor?" he grunted. "Heard you were. But you've got to grow a few more inches, Shorty, and learn better holds than whatever it was you just tried to pull."

I said nothing, but I was doing a lot of thinking. If Max and his friends got away with bullying us this time, they'd try it again. They had to be stopped . . . now.

But I was on the bottom . . .

"You going to play with us like a good boy, or do I have to —" Max started to say, when I made my move. Gathering all the strength I could, I rolled over and pulled Max after me. I did it all so quickly I surprised him. For just a couple of seconds I had broken his hold and was on top of him again, grabbing his left arm and pulling it over his back in a hammerlock.

I'd started to wrestle in school only last year, but I wasn't too bad at it, for a beginner. Being short for my age, it was the one sport that I could get into and really excel at.

I had Max where I wanted him, but again for only a few seconds. He grunted and cursed as he twisted and bolted. Then he squirmed out of my hold and had *me* in a hammerlock.

"Thought you had me, huh?" he snorted, yanking on my arm so hard it hurt. "You giving up, or you want a little more of this?"

"Let him alone, Rundel!" I heard Carl yell out. "You're hurting him!"

I glanced at Carl and saw him clutched between Nyles and McNeer. Both guys had his arms pinned to his sides.

"I am, huh?" Max sneered. "Well, let me hear him say that. Okay?"

"Okay. Okay," I said, feeling the pain all the way up my arm.

He let go of me and pushed down hard on my back as he rose to his feet. I lay there a few seconds, waiting for the pain in my arms and legs to ease up. By the time I felt better and was on my feet, Max was riding my bike down the street. The other two guys were on Carl's bike, with Nyles steering.

There go our bikes, I thought. We'll never see them again, not after that fight. If Max had enough nerve to take on Carl and me in the middle of the street in broad daylight, what would stop him from keeping the bikes?

"You're a fool, Sean, you know that?" Carl snarled at me. "It's a wonder he didn't break your arm!"

I looked at him. According to Mom I was temperamental and headstrong. She had reminded me of that a dozen times, saying that I couldn't control myself, that I got into fights with the least provocation. Well, maybe that was true. But one thing I wasn't was a fool, and I resented Carl's remark.

"I'm no coward," I said, angrily. "And I'm not going to let anyone take my bike without a fi—"

Just then something glittering on the grass caught my eye. It was Max's button, the one that said I AM KING.

I picked it up, wiped the dirt off it, and stuck it into my pocket.

Carl frowned. "You're not going to keep that, are you?" he said. "That's Max's button. You'd better give it back to him if you know what's good for you."

I locked eyes with him. "Yes, I *am* going to keep it," I said firmly.

"Why? You want to get in more trouble?" he snapped.

"If you don't say anything to him he won't know I've got it," I said, trying to keep my cool.

He kept staring at me.

"I might give it back to him sometime. But not now."

"Why not?"

"Because I don't think he deserves it," I said, determined to keep my word. "He's no king. If he can ever prove he's a king, I'll give it back to him."

"You're really an idiot," Carl said, shaking his head.

I shrugged. "You think what you want to think," I said calmly.

Carl was a lot like his father, my stepfather. Neither of them cared for me very much. As a matter of fact, I sometimes felt that there was even a gap between Mom and me, or she wouldn't get on my back for every little mistake I made. Sure, I'd clobbered a few kids who had made fun of my height, but I couldn't just stand back and take it, could I?

"You're just too impetuous," Mom had once said. "You can't control yourself. At the slightest notion you want to drop everything and fight. I sure hope you'll grow up one of these days, Sean — if not physically, at least mentally — and straighten up into a decent young man your father and I can be proud of."

Sure, I thought. And let my name be muddied all the time I was growing and straightening up. Why couldn't anyone see things from my point of view? It was no wonder I felt lonely most of the time, as if something — or someone — was missing from my life.

Mom and my natural father had divorced when I was about two years old, too long ago for me to remember what my father looked like. Mom rarely spoke about him. It was as if there was something about him she didn't want me to know.

Once she did say that he had wrestled in high

school. I guess that may have been one of the reasons I took up the sport. It was something I could do to remind me of him once in a while.

Maybe things would be different if he were still around.

I started to walk homeward, because I felt sure I wouldn't see our bikes again. Wait until Mom and Dad hear about this, I thought. What punishment would Mom impose on me this time? Because she was usually the one who handed out the punishments, not Dad.

A car hummed by. A minute later I heard the sound of our bikes' motors and saw Rundel, Nyles, and McNeer riding down the street toward us. I stared, surprised and relieved to see our bikes again. The guys pulled up in front of us, shut off the engines, and got off the bikes, all sober and innocent-looking, as if this was something they did every day.

"Nice wheels," Max chortled. "Thanks for the ride."

I didn't say anything. Neither did Carl. Apparently neither Max nor his cronies had missed the button that was gone from his shirt.

They turned and headed up the street, Max

in the middle, swaggering like a real kingpin. Suddenly Max turned around, grinned, and waved. The anger I felt about their taking our bikes for a ride around the block came to a boiling point.

"Grin, Punkhead," I muttered. "It's your last time. And the last time you'll ever take our bikes, too."

"Oh, yeah?" Carl said. "How are you going to stop them, Peewee? You going to grow a foot in a week and take on all three?" He laughed.

"No, I'm not going to grow a foot," I said, watching the guys get smaller in the distance. "But I'm going to grow all right."

2

We checked the bikes for damage, but there wasn't any. Our bikes were twins, except for the color. Carl's was white with black trim; mine was red with white trim. They were YZ50s. Dad had given them to us on Carl's twelfth birthday. He'd gotten a pretty good deal on them because he was maintenance manager of a bike shop.

We put on our helmets, got on our bikes, and headed for home.

"You wouldn't have gotten into a fight, you know, if you'd kept your mouth shut," Carl ranted. "I don't know what made you think you could handle those guys. Each one of 'em is twice your size! Don't you have a brain in your head?"

15

"They were trying to take our bikes," I said evenly. "That's what I was thinking about, not sizes."

"Sure. And you saw what happened."

This kind of exchange between Carl and me wasn't new. He'd been on my back ever since he was eight or nine, when he began to grow up like a weed, and I was ten or eleven and hardly growing at all. He'd call me Peewee, or Squirt, or Shorty, more often than by my real name. Why, I didn't know. Maybe it was because he resented having a stepbrother. Maybe it was because he was bigger than me and got a kick out of flaunting it. He wasn't much of a fighter, but when we wrestled on the living room floor he'd beat me every time.

He grumbled on, but I ignored him and got to thinking about Max and his two friends. They went to Franklin Junior High, not far from Jefferson Davis Junior High, where Carl and I went. There'd always been a rivalry between their school and ours. Baseball, football, wrestling — it made no difference. Whenever the two schools got together in any sport it was *war*.

16

We reached home, rode up the concrete driveway to the double garage, and got off our bikes.

"I suppose you're going to spill the beans to Mom," I said to Carl as he lifted the left-side door.

He looked at my pants and jersey. "I won't have to," he observed. "One look at your clothes and she'll know you've been in another fight."

I stared down at my dirt-smudged clothes. "Great," I said. "I guess I'm in for it again." Disgusted, I pushed my bike inside the garage and yanked down the kickstand. What would my punishment be this time? No TV for a week, or maybe two?

As soon as we entered the house, Carl's prediction came true. "For Pete's sake, Sean! You've been fighting again? Look at your clothes!" Mom cried.

Carl and I looked at each other, waiting to see who would talk first. I kept mum.

"Well?" she said, glancing back and forth at us. "Which one of you is going to tell me?"

I took a deep breath and sighed. "You're right, Mom," I said. "*I* got into a fight."

"With whom?"

"Max Rundel, the new kid, and two of his buddies," Carl cut in. "They wanted to borrow our bikes. I wouldn't have minded it, but —" He paused and looked at me.

"And what did you say, Sean?"

"I said no, and they forced us off our bikes," I said. "That's when it started."

"There wouldn't have been a fight if he'd kept his cool and not been a wiseguy," Carl said disgustedly.

"Why, you chick—!" I started to cry out, then stopped. My hands were balled into fists. I felt like slugging him. At the same time I tried hard to control my temper. Getting into a fight with Carl was the last thing I needed to do, especially in front of Mom.

"Okay, okay, cool it!" Mom said sharply. She grabbed me by the shoulder and looked at me hard. "Sean, I don't know what I'm going to do with you. I've warned you a dozen times about fighting, but I might as well have been talking to the wall."

"Mom, those guys took our bikes!" I cried,

raising my voice to make sure she'd hear my side. "How'd I know they'd bring them back? I couldn't just stand there —"

"You didn't think they'd take a chance on getting caught with two stolen bikes, did you?" she snapped back. "I'm sure they're smart enough to realize that they could be arrested. Why, just their taking the bikes for a ride around the block is enough cause for us to press charges. But we're not going to do that. I don't want to make trouble."

She paused for a few seconds to catch her breath, and I wondered if she was thinking about my father. According to her, he used to get into fights, too. But maybe, like me, he'd had his reasons.

"Let's forget it for now and be thankful that neither of you got hurt," she said, her voice calmer. "Shake hands. Remember, you're brothers."

We did as we were told. Carl's grip was as limp as a dead fish.

Then Mom pushed us toward the hallway. "Get out of those clothes, and take a shower," she ordered. "And forget all this foolishness."

Carl looked back at her. "You going to tell Dad?"

"In my own way, in my own time," she answered. "Go. Get changed and showered."

"You first," I said to Carl.

A half an hour later I was lying on my bed with only my shorts on, staring at the white ceiling. Crazy thoughts rambled through my mind. Carl had done it again. He had socked the whole blame for the fight on me. He *was* a coward.

I wondered how I would have turned out if I'd gone to live with my real father instead of with my mother. I'd still be a shorty, but at least I wouldn't have a brother like Carl who'd put me down almost every time he spoke to me.

I got to thinking about my real father, imagining what he looked like, what kind of guy he was. Did he have brown hair and brown eyes like mine? Was he short, tall, or just medium-sized? Did he like the outdoors? Was he a sportsman? Or was he a couch potato? Mom had told me little about him, and that little wasn't good. He had a tendency to get drunk and lose his temper. Once he'd been cut by a beer bottle in a barroom fight.

"That's the reason for our divorce," she'd said one day. "And why I have you and he doesn't."

Then she'd quickly gotten up and gone into the next room, wiping her eyes. I'd decided then that I wouldn't ask her questions about my natural father again.

But I couldn't help thinking about him every once in a while. Maybe, I thought, if I were with him he wouldn't drink as much. Maybe he would have cut it out altogether if a judge had ordered him to. Then again, if he was an alcoholic . . .

I rolled over onto my stomach and buried my face in the pillow. My throat ached. At least Mom cared about me. That much I was sure of. Dad was okay, but he wasn't the hugging kind like Mom. Now and then he'd smile and rub my head when something pleased or amused him, but that was as much as he ever showed his emotions.

He was friendlier toward Carl. I rationalized that Carl was his natural son, but I often wished that he'd show more affection toward me, too.

A voice interrupted my thoughts. Mom was calling me.

I rolled off the bed and opened the door. "Yes?"

"You're wanted on the phone," she said, looking up at me from the bottom of the stairs. "I think it's Adam. And you'd better put on some clothes!"

"Tell him I'll be right there," I said.

I pulled on my pants and shirt and ran barefoot down the carpeted stairs.

"Hi, Bull. What's up?" His name was Adam Cornish, but everybody called him Bull. One look at him and you'd know why.

"I . . . ah . . . Look, I don't want to talk about this over the phone, okay? Can you come over?" He sounded nervous.

I frowned. Seldom had I seen Bull bothered by anything. "Yeah, I'll come over. Soon as I put on my socks and shoes."

3

I biked over to Bull's house and found him sitting on the front porch, petting Nick, his cocker spaniel. The minute Nick saw me coming he scrambled down the short flight of steps and started to bark.

"Pipe down, will you?" I grunted as I rode into Bull's driveway. "Don't you know me yet, for crying out loud? I'm your old buddy, Sean."

He stopped barking, sniffed at my bike and my shoes, then followed me to the steps, his tail wagging like crazy.

"So what's wrong?" I said to Bull. He was sitting against a post, his stomach in three rolls underneath a red T-shirt. He had taken up wrestling two years ago, but seemed to have gained fat instead of muscles.

"Had a fight with the Octopus," he said.

"What? You, too?"

He looked at me. "You had a fight with him, too?"

"Yes. Less than three hours ago." I explained what happened.

"Well, he took my skateboard," Bull said. "That is, he and the monkeys that were with him took it. He wouldn't have done it alone."

I'd seen Bull on his skateboard. You'd think it would bend under his heavy weight, but it doesn't. Still, taking it out from under him would not be an easy feat.

"He's asking for trouble," I said.

"And gets it without trouble," Bull replied.

I socked Bull on the arm, and smiled. "Don't worry. One of these days he'll meet his match."

"Yeah? Who?"

I put my forefinger against my chest.

"You?" Bull laughed. "You must be kidding."

"Just wait and see."

"I'll be an old man by then."

I laughed.

"Maybe we can gang up on him and those two monkeys," Bull suggested. "We can pick up five or six guys and fight them, can't we?"

"Have a gang fight?" I shook my head. "The next thing you know someone will start carrying a knife. Or even a gun. No, there's got to be another way."

Bull shrugged. "I hope you're right. Want some iced tea?"

"Eenie meenie minie mo. Okay," I said.

He went into the house and came back out with two glasses of iced tea. He handed me one and I took a couple of swallows. The tea was unsweetened and tasted rotten. But I didn't tell him that.

"Did you see who you're wrestling this Thursday?" Bull asked after he took a swallow of his.

"Yeah. Bud Luckman."

Bull shook his head. "Wrong. I had to take Dad's lunch to him, 'cause he's working tonight, and I saw the new schedule," he explained. Bull's father was the custodian at our school. "You're wrestling the Squasher and I'm tangling with Jim Byers."

"Nyles? The Octopus's right-hand man?"

"Right."

I frowned. "Why the change?"

Bull shrugged. "I don't know. Maybe Bud's got the flu. It's going around, you know."

"Yeah, I know."

I thought back to that afternoon's incident. Apparently Nyles hadn't known about the change either, or I'm sure he would have said something — a complimentary remark like, "Can't wait to get you on the mat, Shorty."

I got up. "Don't worry about Max, Bull," I said. "We'll take care of him and his friends when we meet on the mat. See you Monday." I petted Nick awhile, then left.

Even though our wrestling teams worked out from 3:30 to 6:30 every day after school, I still exercised at home all the next week. I was determined to build up my body — all five-feet-two of it — as much as I possibly could.

Dad had bought Carl and me a couple of exercise mats, and two seven-pound barbells each. That way we didn't have to worry about conflicts.

"You think all that extra exercise is going to do you any good against the Octopus?" Carl said to me Tuesday when I had finished working out and was ready to shower. "You'd better figure out a way to grow four or five more inches, pal. That would be your only chance. Your *only* chance," he repeated.

"Thanks for the compliment, pal," I said. *You stinkpot,* I wanted to add.

I'm glad I didn't. Things were rough enough between us. It would be stupid to make it worse.

I could've reminded him that Coach Collins had taken a particular interest in me, too. The head coach, Joe Doran, was devoting most of his time to the varsity wrestling squad, letting his assistant, Chad Collins, handle the junior varsity.

"You're wrestling Hunter Nyles this Thursday, you know," Coach Collins had reminded me that afternoon as he started to show me a new hold. I was in my wrestling uniform — full-length tights with outside short trunks, wrestling shoes, and headgear. He was wearing just a sweatshirt with JEFFERSON DAVIS J. H. on it. "The Squasher," he added, grinning. "But

27

you could change that name if you learn a couple of new holds and pull them on him."

"Have you seen him?" I said. "He's almost a foot taller than I am."

"Yes, I've seen him. But, so what? He's thin, and he only tops you by about three or four pounds. You could beat him. I know you could. But you've got to believe that, too."

I smiled. "I know. I've heard that before."

He smiled back, and I noticed a deep wrinkle form above his left eyebrow. He was about four or five inches taller than me, but not as muscular as most wrestling coaches I've seen.

"Okay, let's go to work," he said. "Let's get into starting position. I'll get on the bottom."

He got down on his hands and knees and I got down beside him, putting my right arm across his back and bringing it around to his stomach. Then I gripped his left arm with my right hand.

"Okay," he said. "Just imagine you're the Squasher and I'm you. The referee says 'Ready! Go!' "

In a wink of an eye he rolled over, pulling

me with him. Before I knew it my back was on the floor and his back was on my chest. He had my right leg caught up in a hold I couldn't get out of. He turned, his face only inches from mine, and grinned.

"Got it?" he said.

He was pressing me hard enough to stifle my breathing a little.

"Yeah," I said, almost inaudibly.

He let go of my leg. "That's called the shoulder roll," he said. "It's nothing new, but if done right it works. Okay. You get down this time."

I did, and we went through the roll. I managed to roll him over almost as easily as he had rolled me, and I felt good — until the fourth time we did it. That time he stopped me cold before I could even grab his left leg, and I realized then that he had been letting me go through the entire hold without any strong opposition so that I could learn its execution.

The next day he taught me the hammerlock hold and the legal and the illegal ways of applying it. I had learned how to perform it last year, but not well enough to use it successfully during matches. As he showed me how to do it properly and effectively, I felt as if I were learning it for the first time.

"How you apply it makes a difference," he said. "It's easy to pull it off illegally and lose a point or two. You can put pressure on the upper arm, but putting pressure on the elbow is a no-no. Get it?"

I nodded. "I think so," I said.

"Okay. I want you to work on those two holds, plus the ones you already know," he suggested. "Work out with Bull. I know you two are close friends, so be sure neither of you does anything to hurt yourselves. Work out with your brother, too. Carl's got both height and weight over you, so practicing those holds on him would be pretty beneficial. For both of you." He smiled again. "Don't worry. I'll tell them you're coming."

He glanced around the gym, where groups of guys were doing exercises on the equipment and other groups were practicing wrestling on the mats. Coach Doran was doing his bit with the varsity heavyweights.

"Bull!" Coach Collins yelled out. "Drop that barbell and come here!"

Bull came over, glistening with sweat. Coach Collins explained that he wanted us to work out together, and briefed him on the two holds he had taught me. "I could've let you be surprised," he said, "but I think that your being prepared for the holds might be better practice for Sean. Okay, go to it."

Bull and I went at it, me going down first with Bull on top of me, and I almost got a takedown first thing. But not quite. Bull rolled over onto me, tried to put a headlock on me, and I squirmed and twisted and bounced to my feet before he could get a good hold.

We grinned at each other. I think I surprised him. As a matter of fact, I surprised myself! Bull's a big kid!

"Let's try it again," Coach Collins said.

We did, and I felt strong and in control as I rolled and tumbled with Bull, using the new moves and holds. Bull was good, but I was faster. There were even moments when I thought I was even *better*.

And maybe I was right! I finally got a take-down!

"Sure, you would," Bull said, breathing hard as he rose to his feet, sweat rolling down his cheeks. "I'm bushed!"

I laughed. "I figured," I said.

4

I hardly slept a wink Wednesday night —
squirming and turning and sweating like a pig
about to be butchered — and by Thursday
night I was ready more for a good night's sleep
than for a wrestling match with one of Franklin
Junior High's best.

Hunter Nyles didn't get his nickname, the
Squasher, by squashing melons or oranges. He
got it from squashing his opponents. He was
bigger than me and had wrestled since he was
ten years old. Everything was in his favor.

I was in the 125-pound weight class. I
weighed in at 122 and Nyles at 125.

I tried to ignore the crowd that filled the seats
of the gym. Somewhere among the spectators

sat Mom and Carl. It was funny — Mom was behind me all the way when it came to wrestling, even though my real father had been a wrestler. I guess she thought it was a good way for me to get out my frustrations — and stay out of trouble. Dad didn't attend the matches. Tallying up the week's receipts absorbed his time Thursday nights. I wondered why he couldn't do them some other time, but I'd never asked him.

As for Carl, he'd cheer quicker for Bull than he would for me.

We stood outside of the mat, Hunter Nyles on one side and I on the other. Bob Townsend, the ref, a tall, balding guy with a barrel chest, stepped onto the mat. The red and green armbands on his wrists made it easier for the scorekeeper to see which wrestler had scored when the ref raised his hand to indicate a point. In this match the green, on his right wrist, represented Jefferson Davis Junior High, since the meet was being held at our school.

The assistant referee, Clint Wagner, a muscular guy who had a trim mustache and was only a couple of inches taller than me, stood on the opposite side of the mat, watching. He, too, wore armbands.

"Okay, Jefferson. On the mat," Referee Townsend said.

I got on the mat. Then Nyles. We stood apart, facing each other, waiting for the ref to blow his whistle. I was scared. Nyles looked even bigger in his tights than he did in his everyday clothes. He might be thin, like Coach Collins said, but he wasn't *that* thin.

Shreeeek!

The whistle blew and we went at it, grabbing each other's hands and releasing them. Suddenly Nyles grabbed my hands again, rushed at me, and dived at my legs, pulling me toward him as he did so. I could hear him grunt as I went down, falling on my back. He pressed his head against my stomach, fighting for a quick takedown, and I squirmed and twisted to keep him from doing so.

It did no good. From the corner of my eye I saw the ref raise two fingers. I winced. Two points already for the Squasher!

I gritted my teeth, rolled over, and got an arm around Nyles's neck. He squirmed out of it as if he were greased. I was positive then that there was more to this skinny kid than what filled his tights.

I twisted around to face him. I was down, with my left leg straight out and my right curved under me, when he got his arms around my waist and locked his hands against my chest. I could feel the tight pressure of his skinny arms. They felt like ropes cutting into my body. I could hear and feel him breathing hard against my neck. I thought I was a goner for sure when, suddenly, I saw the ref lean forward and tap Nyles's arm.

The Squasher released me instantly, and the ref straightened up and made the locked-hands violation sign over his head for the scorekeeper to see. Then a finger flashed.

A point for me!

In a moment we were in tight combat again, the Squasher diving at my legs as I stood up. I grabbed his head and rolled over onto the mat, pulling him with me. He squirmed out of my control and wrapped his hand over my neck in a half nelson. It was a takedown. Two more points for him.

A second later I twisted out of his grasp and tried the shoulder roll on him, as Coach Collins had taught me. A cheer exploded from the Jefferson Davis gallery, and I knew I'd scored two points for a reversal. But, like a slippery eel, Nyles twisted out of my grasp and got an armlock around my leg. Another point for him.

A whistle shrilled, ending the first period. We broke apart and stood up, breathing hard and sweating like crazy. I glanced at the scorer.

"Five points for Nyles! Three points for Bailor!" he announced.

In spite of the Squasher's leading by only two points, I was nervous and tight. Sweat rolled down my face, arms, and legs in rivers. I was afraid that the next time we got into a clinch he'd pull some quick, secret move and pin me. I could picture him gloating down at me. *Next time have your coach pick out a guy your size, Halfpint.*

I couldn't let him think like that. I *had* to show him that just because I was smaller I was no pushover. If he was going to best me, he'd really have to earn the win, and maybe the next time the tide would change.

The second period started and we went at it. It didn't start off well — the Squasher got a single-leg hold on me almost before I was ready. Then he was penalized again for putting an illegal chicken wing hold on me. Seconds later he clasped a hand over my mouth and started to twist my head, a no-no, just as a hand-over-nose or -throat would be, and he lost another point.

His breaking the rules made me realize how desperate he was. He had found out that I was tougher than he'd thought, and that he had to play dirty to score. I just hoped the ref wouldn't miss any of it.

I tried the shoulder roll again. This time I pulled it off. I felt better. I almost grinned in his face. Some of the tension left. If I could do it once I could do it again, I thought.

I tried, but the Squasher twisted out of my hold and rolled me over onto my back, winning points for a near fall. I strained with all my power as he tried to pin me. His left arm was holding down my left leg and his right arm was wrapped around my neck. But I was up on my elbows, straining hard, and he couldn't budge me.

We split points in the third period, he getting four more than I. The match ended with him scoring sixteen points to my ten. Three points for his team.

We shook hands and looked at each other eye to eye. He'd won, but he wasn't happy. I could tell by the disappointed look on his perspiring face. He had thought I was going to be easy pickin's, that he'd pin me.

Well, he didn't. And if there was a next time . . .

Oh, heck, I thought. I'll wait until the next time came. The important thing was *now*. I wasn't afraid of him anymore. Not a bit.

"Good show, Sean," Coach Collins said as he met me outside of the mat with a broad smile on his face. He shook my hand, put an arm around my shoulders, and gave me a squeeze. "You gave him a battle."

"Thanks, Coach," I said.

"You need more work on the roll," he added.

"And a couple of other holds. But don't worry. You did okay, even if you did lose. Not only is that Nyles kid bigger than you are, he's also more experienced. I hope you don't feel bad about coming out on the short end."

I winced at the coach's pun. "Not too bad," I answered truthfully. I really hadn't expected to get within ten points of the Squasher, let alone six.

Neither Mom nor Carl looked half as pleased as the coach had.

"I can't understand why they put that big kid against you," Mom complained. "Don't they match you boys up by size?"

There you go, I thought, bringing up "size" again. It would never end.

"By weight, Mom," I said, trying to shrug off my irritation. "He only weighed a few pounds more than I did."

"Mom's right," Carl cut in. "I think you're lucky he didn't make hamburger out of you."

Thanks, brother, I thought. He still enjoyed ridiculing me. Would his digs never end, either?

"Anyway, you did okay," Mom said. "Bigger

41

or not, that Nyles boy showed he had more experience. In a couple of years — maybe even next year — you'll give him a run for his money, I'm sure."

I smiled and shrugged. "Maybe," I said.

"Wish I was old enough to wrestle with the JV's," Carl said. "I bet I could handle most of those characters."

"I wish you were old enough, too," I said.

I meant it. Maybe a good wrestling match with some of those "characters" would teach him something about humility.

I took a shower, got into my civvies, and started to head back to the gym when two girls came dashing around the corner. The first one crash-banged right into me.

"Oh! I'm sorry!" she cried, grabbing my shoulder to catch her balance.

"That's okay," I said, reaching out to catch my balance, too.

She pushed back ringlets of her blond hair and stared at me with wide, grapelike eyes. "Oh! You're Sean, aren't you? Sean Bailor? You just wrestled Hunter Nyles."

I nodded. "Yes. And lost."

42

"Oh, but it wasn't such a bad loss," she said. "I thought you did fine."

"Yeah. Me, too," the girl next to her said.

This other girl had shoulder-length brown hair and wore a sweatshirt that had a picture of Garfield the cat on the front. Were they just being nice to me? I wondered. They were probably students of Franklin Junior High. I'd never seen them before.

"I'm Gail and she's Barbara," the blonde said. She flashed a smile and waved. "Nice meeting you! See you again — maybe!"

They ran off, heading toward the far side of the stands where the Franklin Junior High students and fans were sitting.

Some of the Jefferson Davis fans yelled and waved as I headed down the gym, and I waved back.

Suddenly I heard my name. "Sean!"

I paused. It was the assistant referee, Clint Wagner.

"Got a minute?" he asked.

5

He was sitting close to the scorekeepers' table. "Have a seat," he said, patting the vacant space beside him.

I sat down, wondering what he wanted me for.

"Referees aren't in a position to take an interest in kids they referee," he said. "But I think we have something in common. Right?"

I shrugged. I could see only one thing we had in common.

"Our height?" I guessed.

"Right. And since I'm only an assistant ref, I don't have to worry about expressing an opinion that might show prejudice. So I think it's perfectly okay for me to give you a few point-

44

ers," he went on. "That is, if you don't mind."

I looked at him, a little surprised. "No, I don't mind," I said.

Why should I? I was willing to accept any help I could get, especially from an assistant referee! That was just one hat he wore. During the daytime he worked at Wolcott's Hardware Store. I'd first seen him there about six months ago.

"We've only got a couple of minutes before the next match starts," he observed, glancing at the scoreboard clock. "But I wanted to ask you if you'd mind if we got together sometime so I could teach you a few moves and holds. You show potential. I think I can make you a good wrestler. Maybe a champion wrestler."

He paused, probably to let his words sink into my head. When they did, they made my heart pound. Me, a champion? Well, why not? Why not, if I really trained for it?

"We're not giants, but I'm sure you took up wrestling for the same reasons I did. It's an individual sport, one on one. What we do, we do on our own. It's also a good body-building exercise, and it teaches you some valuable

45

traits, especially self-reliance and initiative. But we must learn and improve."

I smiled. It was funny getting a lecture out of the blue, but it was nice, too. I appreciated the fact that he, Clint Wagner, whom all the kids liked, had taken an interest in my wrestling. We'd known each other for some time, but it wasn't until now — wrestling season — that he really talked to me.

He paused. "I like your style, Sean. And you've got guts. Whether you let me or anyone else help you, I don't think you should ignore your potential. Know what I mean?"

I nodded. "I sure do. And I'd definitely be interested, Mr. Wagner."

A whistle shrieked. It was time for the next match.

He got up and headed for the mat. For a moment I sat there, feeling kind of special and honored. Then I took a deep breath, stood up, and searched the stands for Mom and Carl.

"Sean!" a shrill voice piped up.

I turned in the direction of the voice and saw a hand, with a bracelet sparkling on its wrist, waving like crazy. Then the waving

46

changed to a beckon. It was Gail. With her was Barbara.

I stood there, considering the invitation.

I saw another hand waving and I recognized Mom. Carl was with her, but his attention was on the match taking place on the floor.

I waved to her, then raised five fingers and mouthed the words "Five minutes," while I pointed toward Gail and Barbara.

I squeezed between two shoulders and climbed up to where the girls were sitting. Gail had pressed up against Barbara and was patting the empty space beside her, smiling broadly.

"Thanks for coming!" she said.

"You're welcome," I said.

I sat down beside her, and something dropped out of my pocket. It was Max's I AM KING button. I quickly picked it up and jammed it back into my pocket, hoping neither of the girls had seen it. But then again, if they did, so what? It wouldn't mean anything to them.

I looked down at the gym floor and saw that none other than the Octopus, Max Rundel, was wrestling with Dick Treman, our best in the

47

125-pound class. I cringed as I saw Rundel whirl Dick over onto his back and get on top of him in a crossbody ride, pulling up Dick's left arm, which might've turned into a potentially dangerous hold if he hadn't let go of the arm and spun onto Dick's back.

Both girls started to jump up and down, clap, and shout like crazy.

"You two wouldn't happen to be from Franklin, would you?" I said, grinning at Gail.

She laughed. "How can you tell?"

"You're cheering for the Octopus. And nobody would cheer for him unless they were from the same school."

Her laughter faded. "Oh? Do you know him?"

"*Know* him?" I was about to tell her about what had happened between us a week earlier, but then I changed my mind. How did I know that they weren't good friends of Rundel's? It was best that I kept my mouth shut. "Yeah, I know him," I said, my tone of voice suggesting that I wasn't elated about it. "But I think I'll know him better one of these days."

She looked at me with those large eyes.

"What do you mean? Oh, that you two might wrestle each other?"

I nodded. "We might."

"*You?*" Barbara cried, sizing me up and down. "You and Max?"

I could tell what she was thinking.

"I wouldn't be surprised," I said. "I may be short, but we both wrestle in the same weight class."

"Oh, no!" Barbara moaned, as if the Octopus and I getting together in a wrestling match would be like Rambo going up against Mickey Mouse. "That can't be! It wouldn't be fair!"

"Why not?" Gail said, turning toward her. "Don't you think Max is beatable?"

"Yes, but . . ." Barbara leaned forward to look at me, sizing me up again to make sure her first evaluation was correct. She didn't have to say anything more.

"Size has got something to do with it," Gail admitted, "but not everything. It takes guts, too. And Sean's got a lot of that, in my opinion."

I laughed. "Thanks, Gail," I said. I could've hugged her, but I didn't have the nerve. After all, we'd just met.

Suddenly, there was a loud cheer and I saw the ref put up an arm — the one with a green band on it — and raise a finger. A point for Dick Treman. Hooray for the home team.

Moments later, however, the Octopus surprised him with a half nelson and pinned him.

Both girls cheered, Barbara much louder than Gail. I wondered why she wasn't down on the floor with the Franklin JV cheerleaders. She certainly had the enthusiasm — and the voice — for it.

I sat with the girls about five minutes longer, then excused myself. I said I hoped to see them again, looking directly at Gail as I said it, and they both promised that I would.

I found Mom and Carl, and we watched Bull win his match with no problems at all, scoring the most points of any of us, which was no surprise.

Later, after he'd showered and dressed, Bull came up into the stands and squeezed in beside me. After watching a couple of ninety-eight-pounders go at it for a while, Bull said, "How about you and me going home by ourselves? We'll stop at Hungry Mike's and I'll treat."

"Sure." I seldom refused Bull's offers to treat me, and he *never* refused my treating him.

I got permission from Mom, and we left. The matches were almost finished, anyway. We walked about two blocks to Hungry Mike's, split a submarine sandwich, exchanged expert opinions about the match for about ten minutes, then left. It was about a quarter of ten, and a cool breeze was chilling the air. I pulled the collar of my light jacket tighter around my neck.

"This is the kind of night I like," Bull said, the bright red light of the Hungry Mike's sign flashing on his face. "Cool, quiet, and lazy."

The breeze was teasing his hair and ruffling the sides of his open windbreaker. "Lazy?" I echoed.

"Yeah." Then Bull stiffened. He stared down the street, his mouth parted. I looked in the same direction, and my mouth dropped open, too.

"I guess I spoke too soon," Bull whispered.

"Okay, Runt," Max Rundel blurted, stepping up to me from the night shadows. "My button.

Hand it over, or you know what's coming to you."

In the soft light behind him I could see his left- and right-hand buddies, Hunter "the Squasher" Nyles and John McNeer.

"What button?" I said.

I knew what button, but I wasn't about to hand it over to him.

How did he know about it, anyway? I hadn't told him, and I knew Carl hadn't.

He grabbed me by the collar of my jacket and stared down at me, his eyes on fire. I could feel his breath as he snapped at me, "Don't give me that bull, Shortfry! Barbara told me she saw it fall out of your pocket! Hand it over! Now!"

I was sick. So Barbara *had* seen the button when I dropped it. I didn't want to think that she got me in trouble on purpose. Maybe she didn't know it belonged to Max and had mentioned it to him without thinking.

I grabbed his wrist with both of my hands and tried to loosen his hold. He hung on like a vise.

Bull stepped up to him. "Let him alone, Rundel," he ordered. "If he's got a button it's his, not yours."

"Out of the way, Bull Durham," Max quipped, without taking his eyes off me, "or these two guys behind me will mop up the street with you."

"Is that so?"

Bull started to rush at Max.

"No, Bull!" I cried, putting out a hand to stop him. "Keep out of this!"

He paused in his tracks, just as Nyles and McNeer ran up to him, each grabbing him by an arm.

Max, still holding the collar of my jacket, poked me in the stomach with his other fist and snarled, "You gonna give it to me, or do I have to take it from you?"

Pain shot through my stomach. That did it. I had to defend myself, no matter how much bigger he was.

I closed both of my hands together and drove them as hard as I could against Max's arm. He let go, and I heard him grunt. I knew the blow hurt him. It had hurt my left wrist.

In a blink of an eye he ducked his head and dove at me. He struck me with his left shoulder, and I went down like a ton of bricks. My head struck the ground with a crunch, and for a few seconds the night filled up with a million lightning bugs.

I rolled over before I could see clearly again, knowing that if I didn't he would jump on me and probably put a hold on me — legal or illegal, it made no difference here. Maybe he'd injure me enough to knock me out of wrestling for a while. I didn't want that.

I started to jump to my feet, but lost my balance as he grabbed my left leg and yanked me down. I hit the ground again, and a ball of lead — that's what it felt like — struck me on the thigh. The pain shot up my whole left side.

I swung a fist at him and missed.

Then he grabbed my arm and twisted it into a wristlock, putting on pressure that caused pain to shoot up my arm. I wanted to scream with pain, but I didn't. I wasn't going to give the Octopus the satisfaction.

Suddenly I saw a figure loom up behind him and grab his arms. Instantly the pain stopped

54

as Max released my arm and wrist. The figure pulled him away and hung onto him, despite Max's trying to shake himself loose.

Silhouetted against the sky the figure looked familiar.

"Okay, you guys," his voice — familiar, too — cut in. "Break it up. Fast."

6

"Smart hold that was, but illegal. And you knew it, didn't you?" Clint Wagner said to Max. "You only use a wristlock when your legal moves don't work. And I can't say I saw you use any of those on Sean."

I rose to my feet, wondering: How long had he been watching us before he'd decided to break up our fight?

Max looked at him. His jaw muscles moved, but he kept his mouth clamped shut.

"Okay. Take off. All three of you," Clint ordered, shoving Max toward Nyles and McNeer. "You should've been heading for home, anyway, after those wrestling matches, not hanging around here like street bums. Go on! Scram! Or I'll show you what real wrestling is!"

The three glared at him for a few seconds, then headed down the street past Hungry Mike's, Max looking so angry that he could have chewed leather.

I looked at Clint. "Thanks, Mr. Wagner," I said. "I guess you got here in the nick of time."

He grinned. "You boys want a ride home?"

"I think that's a great idea!" Bull answered, wiping his sweating face with a handkerchief.

Clint led us around the side of the restaurant to his yellow jalopy, and we got in. "What started the fight?" he asked, as we drove out of the parking lot and headed down the street.

Neither Bull nor I said anything for a minute. Finally I told him about my finding Max's button with the words I AM KING on it.

"Why don't you want to give it back to him?"

I shrugged. "I don't know. Maybe I will . . . someday."

Clint grinned at me. "When he proves he is king, right?"

I shrugged again. "The kind of guy he is," I said, "I doubt he can be king of anything."

57

Clint nodded. "Well said, my friend."

We changed the topic and talked about the wrestling matches until we got to Bull's house. Bull thanked Clint for the ride, then I gave Clint my address and we headed for it.

"I just got a terrific idea," he said as he turned down Orange Avenue, my street. "How'd you like to go fishing with me Saturday morning?"

I stared at him. Fishing? I'd never fished in my life! Dad didn't care for it, so I hadn't ever thought about it.

"Sure," I said, "I'd like to. But . . ." I paused, thinking.

"But, what?"

I didn't want to tell him that my father had never taken me. I also wasn't sure Mom would permit it.

"For one thing, I don't have a fishing pole," I said, which was the truth.

He looked at me. Dark tree shadows danced across his face. "Let me guess. You've never fished before, right?"

"Right."

"Oh, you'll love it. One thing about fishing: even if you don't catch anything, it's fun!"

58

I laughed.

"The pole's no problem," he said. "I've got three or four of them. Ask your parents if it's okay — I know you've got to do that — then give me a call Friday night. Okay?"

Why did I feel so good all of a sudden? Why, when I'd met Clint only a few months ago, did it now seem as if I'd known him all my life? He was friendly, sympathetic, and understanding — attributes a kid would expect in his father. Except my father had never shown me those attributes.

I felt a lump come to my throat and took a deep breath. "Okay," I replied. "I'll call you Friday night."

"Great!"

We were driving up to the curb in front of my house when I saw the red taillights of our car wink out in the garage. Had Mom and Carl just arrived home? They should've been home at least half an hour ago. Why were they so late?

The lights were on in the house, so I assumed that Dad was up, probably still doing bookwork or watching television.

I got out of Clint's car just as Mom and Carl came out of the garage. Carl was carrying a sack of groceries. He glanced briefly at us, then turned to pull down the garage door.

Mom stood there like a statue, staring.

"Hi," I said.

"Hi," she murmured.

"Hello!" Clint called out. Then, "Good night!" and I turned in time to see him wave.

"Good night," I called back.

I noticed then that his muffler was loud and clangy, and that the glass of the right taillight was broken. Through the rear window of the jalopy I could see him still waving, and I waved back, feeling good inside. Even Dad had never shown such interest in me in all my life.

I turned and started to head for the house when I saw that Mom was still standing there, watching the jalopy disappear down the darkened street. She had a long, drawn look on her face. A worried look.

"Who was that?" she asked.

"Clint Wagner, the assistant referee," I said.

"Where'd he pick you up?"

I paused and thought hard before I answered her. I hated to admit that I'd been in another fight with the Octopus. For all I knew she'd look up Max's address, go there, and have a verbal fight with his parents. Like me, she had guts.

Just the same I had to come clean. She'd probably find out about it eventually. I cleared my throat and told her about the fight, and about Clint Wagner coming to my rescue.

Mom's anger flared. "Another fight? What am I raising, a hood? Are you going to be a replica of your father and get into a fight everytime you go out on the street?"

"It wasn't like that, Mom," I said, hoping I could make her understand. "I didn't start it. Those guys did."

"Sure! It's always the same excuse! The other guys always start it! It's never you! Your father used to say the same thing! You're just like him! You're both bums!"

She whirled and stormed toward the house.

I was sick. I figured now a fishing trip with Clint was out of the question. I might as well not even ask for permission. I might as well just call up Clint and tell him I couldn't go.

That night I couldn't sleep a wink, thinking about the fight with Max and what Mom had said to me.

"You're just like him! You're both bums!"

What a lousy thing to say.

But I wondered: Will I really end up like my father?

7

"I don't think wrestling's for him, Mom," Carl said at the breakfast table the next morning. "I'm afraid that one of these days he's gonna get hurt, and get hurt bad. Look what happened last night. The Squasher really squashed him."

"What?" I stared at him. He was sitting across from me, pouring cereal into his bowl. "You must be talking about some other match, man. He didn't pin me, did he? And he only beat me by a few points."

"Two more and it would've been a major decision," Carl said. "And four points instead of three."

"But it *wasn't* a major decision, and it *wasn't*

64

four points!" I stormed. "So stop blowing off, okay?"

"Okay, okay," Dad said sharply. "Stop this silly bickering. Eat your breakfast, Carl, and get ready for the bus. That goes for you, too, Sean."

My heart thumped against my ribs as I tried to eat my breakfast and avoid Carl's eyes. When was he going to stop badgering me?

In a minute Dad wiped his mouth with a napkin, excused himself, and kissed Mom. "See you guys later," he said, as he grabbed his jacket and left. Being maintenance manager of Paul's Motorcycle and Bike Shop had him leaving the house first every morning. This ritual went on six days a week, Monday through Saturday. Sometimes I wondered which he loved the most, Mom and us kids — Carl, anyway — or his job.

I stalled finishing my breakfast on purpose. I wanted to talk to Mom. Alone.

I still had a piece of toast left when Carl finished. "Better get a move on, guy," he said as he wiped his mouth and pushed away from the table. "The bus is due here any minute."

"Go ahead," I said. "I'll be out in a sec."

He pulled on his jacket, grabbed up his books, gave Mom a quick peck on the cheek, and left.

"You'd better hurry up, Sean," Mom advised, sitting at the table with a cup of coffee in her hand. "Your brother's right. The bus is due any minute."

I looked at her, my stomach tightening up into a knot. Her hair was bunched on top of her head in a messy-looking bun and her face was pale. But she was calmer than she'd been last night.

"Mom," I said, and paused. A lump caught in my throat.

"Yes? What is it?"

I swallowed the lump. "I — I'm sorry. About the fight and all."

Mom sighed. "I'm sorry, too, for the things I said. It's just that I worry about what will become of you. You're so like your father."

"Well, he must've had *some* good points, or you wouldn't have married him in the first place, right?" I said gently. I was nervous. I

66

didn't think I'd ever be nervous talking to my own mother, but I was. Still, I wanted to know more about my real father.

She shrugged and took a sip of her coffee. "I've told you about him. What else is there to say?"

I could sense she wasn't keen about continuing this conversation. Maybe I was wasting time. I started to get out of my chair.

"He was a decent, good-looking guy when we first met and started dating," she said, and I sat back down. "Then, after we got married, something happened. He changed, became almost a different person. He grew a mustache, then a beard. I didn't object to that. But then he began drinking . . . more."

"That's when he got into fights, too?"

She nodded. "You know the rest," she said.

I had a tough time asking my next question. "Did he want me?"

She glanced at me for a second, then looked away. "He loved you very much," she said, "but he knew it was best that you stay with me. We had no argument about that."

"Did he ever send you any money?"

"Alimony payments, you mean?" She shook her head. "No. Oh, he was willing to, all right. But I refused. I was so angry with him I didn't want a thing to do with him . . . ever. I wanted him completely out of my life."

"You didn't want him to see me?"

She looked at me. "That's right, Sean. I was afraid that if he did, he might change his mind. He might want to take you from me."

"What did he do then? Where did he go?"

"He quit his job and joined one of the armed forces — the army or the navy — I'm not sure which."

Just then there was a yell from outside. It was Carl.

"The bus is here," I said. I got up, kissed Mom on the cheek, and grabbed my jacket. "Thanks, Mom," I said. "See you tonight."

I rushed out the door just as the bus was pulling up to the curb.

"Don't tell me you took all this time finishing up that toast," Carl grunted.

"Okay, I won't," I said.

The door of the bus opened and we got on.

He sat down beside another kid, and I sat a few rows farther back. I was glad we didn't sit together. He might start asking me questions about why I wasn't out sooner. I couldn't tell him what I was talking about with Mom. I would've had to make up some story.

When 3:30 rolled around I, and all the other wrestlers, headed for the locker room. We put on our uniforms and headgear and went out on the mats. I saw both coaches, Joe Doran and Chad Collins, standing with their arms crossed, probably discussing strategy for our upcoming meet next week. I didn't know who our varsity was up against, but we JV's were wrestling guys from Gardner Junior High. They were good, but not great. At least that was what we'd heard through the grapevine.

"Okay, you guys!" Coach Doran yelled out. "Spend some time on the weights! Then we'll team up for some wrestling practice!"

We worked out for about ten minutes, then a whistle shrieked and Coach Doran ordered the varsity to one side of the gym and the junior varsity to the other side. For a moment Coach

Collins studied us like an army master sergeant. Our eyes met, and for a second I thought he was going to call on me.

"Rick," he then said to the kid next to me. "Step out here."

Rick stepped forward, and he and Coach Collins got onto the mat. Rick was a tall, weed-thin kid with arms that looked like long hot dogs, but his size would fool you if you didn't know him. He wrestled in the ninety-eight-pound class and was one of the best.

"I think we need some practice on the half nelson and the leg trap," the coach said. "Most of you guys still don't seem to have gotten the hang of it. Now, keep a close watch on what we do and what I say."

We watched like hawks as he showed us how to apply the half nelson, a move I liked and used whenever I got the opportunity. He worked his far arm under Rick's shoulder. You can work your inside arm under your opponent's near shoulder, too, depending on the situation. The coach moved his outside hand under Rick's armpit and around the top of his neck, brought Rick's arm up and his head down, and put pressure on Rick's shoulder. Then he grabbed Rick's chin with the hand that was around his neck, spread his legs to give him leverage, lay on Rick's chest, and got a pin.

"See how it works?" the coach said, grinning up at us.

We nodded like a bunch of puppets.

Next he showed us the leg trap. Again he had Rick lie on his stomach on the mat and he got on top of Rick, putting his right forearm against Rick's neck and pulling Rick's right leg up with his right knee. It was a good hold, but it took a lot of practice. And that's what we all did when he finished showing us the holds on Rick. We paired off — Bull chose me before I had a chance to pick out anyone else — and we worked on the half nelson first. I got down on the mat and he lay on me. Needless to say, I was glad when we switched positions!

We worked on the move and hold three times, then practiced the leg trap three times.

"I like that!" Bull exclaimed as we climbed to our feet, both of us hot, sweaty, and panting. "Let's go through 'em again!"

71

"Like heck!" I said. "If anybody ought to be called the Squasher, it's you!"

He grinned. "Yea-a-h!" he said.

"Okay. We're going to get into the real meat of things now," Coach Collins said. "A two-minute workout with an opponent other than the guy you practiced with. Dave, you and Smitty get together. Bull, you and Moe. Sean, you and Bud."

Bud and I were in the same weight class. We got on different mats and, when Coach Collins blew the whistle, we went at it. Bud was about two inches taller than me, but in no time at all I grabbed his right leg, floored him, and applied the first hold the coach had us practice: the half nelson. It worked, and I got off him, feeling pretty good.

"Hey! Nice work, Sean!" Coach Collins said, coming over to me. "You pulled off the half like an old pro!"

I shrugged. "I think Bud was tired," I said.

"Not any more tired than you," the coach said.

He tapped me on the head and walked away, still smiling. I felt like an Olympic champ.

The half nelson and the leg trap — a couple of good moves I might be able to use when the Octopus and I clashed.

I felt eager and ready to go. If I didn't change old kid brother Carl's opinion about my wrestling in my next meet, I'd never change it.

I couldn't wait.

8

During supper that night, I made up my mind
to ask Mom and Dad if I could go fishing with
Clint on Saturday. I had apologized, after all,
and it would be a chance for me to try something new and get to know Clint better.

When I finally brought it up they both looked
at me as if I'd asked for a thousand dollars.

"It's no big deal," I said. "And I'll be out of
your hair for a couple of hours."

I didn't know how long we'd be fishing, but
a couple of hours seemed long enough.

"But what do you know about the man?"
Mom asked in the same tone she always used
when she had doubts about my intentions.

"Mom! How much do I have to know?" I exclaimed. "He works at Wolcott's Hardware Store! And he's the assistant referee at school! Everybody thinks he's a great guy!"

That didn't seem to impress her.

"Why did he ask you to go fishing with him?" she pressed.

"He's taken an interest in my wrestling," I said. "I think that's what he'd like to talk about while we're out there."

Carl scoffed. "The guy thinks my brother has po-ten-tial," he said, smiling as he filled his mouth with a forkful of black-eyed peas.

"Maybe he does," Mom said. "But I still don't like the idea."

"I'm fourteen," I said, getting an uncomfortable feeling in my stomach. It wasn't the food. I loved fried chicken, potatoes, and black-eyed peas. It was a knot, getting tighter every minute. "I think you and Dad should trust me by now."

"We do trust you, Sean," Mom said calmly, "but only, I'm sorry to say, up to a point."

"What d'you mean?"

"I mean that you've betrayed that trust more than once by getting into fights when I've warned you not to time and time again. No, I think as punishment I won't let you go fishing. Maybe the next time you feel like slamming your fists into somebody just because they've gotten under your skin you'll remember, and control yourself."

"Mom!" I cried, flabbergasted at her decision.

"That's it!" she said, raising a hand to stop me from saying another word. "That's my answer. No fishing. And that's final."

I was so angry I wanted to yell at her, "Mom, I hate you!" but the words wouldn't come out.

I couldn't eat another morsel. I shoved back my chair and headed upstairs. I could feel Mom's, Dad's, and Carl's eyes riveted on my back, and I thought Mom or Dad would order me to return to the table. But neither did, and I went on to my room.

Mom didn't understand me, that's all there was to it. She wasn't fair inflicting such a severe punishment on me. I didn't deserve it. I'd never fished in my life, and now that I finally had the opportunity to do it, she refused to grant it to me. It was more than a punishment. It was downright mean.

Lying there on my bed, with my hands crossed behind my head, I made a decision. I'd go against Mom's order.

I'd go fishing anyway.

That night, after the rest of the family had gone to bed, I crept downstairs and called Clint. I told him I'd go fishing with him in the morning and would meet him at nine o'clock at the front entrance of the mall.

"I could pick you up at your house," he suggested.

"No," I said. "I've got to pick up something. I'll meet you there. Okay?"

"Okay," he said.

I hung up, feeling guilty, but at the same time feeling kind of thrilled, too. I was going fishing for the first time in my life, with someone — maybe the only person in the world — who really cared about me.

Clint had two fishing poles and a can of worms in the back seat of his jalopy when he picked me up the next morning. He said he had dug up the worms earlier in the back yard of the apartment complex where he lived.

It took us about ten minutes to get to a small lake surrounded by a cluster of woods, a playground, and a park. It wasn't far from Mount Villa College. Mom and Dad had brought us here several times for picnics, but never to fish.

Clint brought out the poles, a can of worms, and a stringer on which to put the fish if we caught any, and we walked out on a dock that stuck out into the lake about twenty feet or so. He showed me how to bait a hook with a wet, squirming worm, then how to reel out the line. After he baited his hook and heaved out his line, we sat on the edge of the dock and waited for the fish to bite.

I still felt guilty. My excuse to Mom this morning had been that I was going to the mall for a while. It was something I often did, so she wouldn't be curious.

Lying to her bothered me, but I felt she wasn't fair. I wasn't going to let her or anybody else push me around. Maybe I *was* just like my father.

I brushed aside my thoughts and concentrated on fishing. I was enjoying every bit of it and hoped I'd catch one or two before we were finished. But I was curious about Clint, too. In a way, Mom was right. I didn't know any more about him than what he did for a living.

After ten minutes or so of not getting even a nibble, I asked him if he was married.

"I *was* married a long time ago," he replied. "But I'm not anymore."

"Oh. I'm sorry," I said.

Did he mean he was divorced, or a widower? I was afraid to ask.

I also hesitated before asking my next question, but I finally did. "Do you have any kids?"

"No. Can't say that I do." He glanced at me and smiled. "I always wanted to have a son. Not that I would have minded having a daughter, you understand. But I guess I wanted a boy because I could wrestle with him. I've always liked wrestling. Was a champ in the navy."

I stared at him. "You were in the navy?"

He nodded. "Six years."

My line stiffened just then and I felt a tug

79

on the pole. "I think I've got one!" I whispered, my heart starting to pound.

He glanced at my line and the pole. "You sure have! Pull it up, then reel 'er in!"

I did, and out of the water squirted a fish about a foot long, its tail whipping every which way.

"Great work, Sean!" Clint cried. "You caught yourself a trout!"

I reeled it in and he showed me how to remove the hook from its throat. Then he slipped it on the stringer, secured one end of it to the dock, and dropped the end with the trout on it into the water.

"My first fish!" I shouted. "I can't believe it!"

"Believe it," Clint said, grinning. "I'm your witness."

We sat there for another fifteen minutes before I got another nibble. But this time no fish. A few minutes later Clint landed one — he said it was a bass.

"We keep this up we'll have enough fish for both of us," he said.

His words hit me like a cannon shot. I guess I must have shown it because he turned to me and asked, "What's the matter? You *are* going to take home some fish if we catch a few, aren't you?"

"I . . . I hadn't thought about it," I said. My insides felt like a tight banjo string for a second.

"You didn't tell your parents you were going fishing with me, did you?"

I took a deep breath and shook my head.

"I thought so," he said. "I thought it was strange that you wanted me to pick you up at the mall instead of at your house. You didn't sound quite like yourself, either. What's wrong? Didn't your parents want you to go fishing with me?"

"My mom didn't," I admitted. "My dad didn't say a word."

Then I told him how my dad didn't care about me, how my mom was so overprotective of me that I lost my cool at times, and how Carl and I couldn't get along. When I was finished I felt as if a ten-ton weight had been lifted from my shoulders. Clint was the first and only person I'd been able to confide in about my problems.

"Don't worry. It'll work out," he said simply.

Sure, I thought. But when?

"Sometimes you just have to wait things out," Clint said, as though he'd read my mind.

Before the two hours were up we had caught five fish, and I'd had more fun than I could remember having in years.

But by the time we decided to pack it in, I was thinking about a lot more than fish. Crazy thoughts, about Clint. He was my size, he was a wrestler, and he had been in the navy. Was it just a coincidence that he had taken an interest in me, or was there some other reason behind it? Maybe he wanted to make up for lost time . . . *maybe Clint Wagner was my real father.*

But why wouldn't he come out and say so? Why would he change his name? And why hadn't he come back before this?

There was only one answer: he was ashamed of his past.

I almost asked him straight out, but I was afraid to. He might say no to keep me from knowing the truth, because of what he used to be: a drunk. He might say no because he was afraid I might want to see him more often, and, if I did, it would cause trouble between Mom and my stepfather. Or he might say no because I was wrong about him. Still, the evidence suggested . . .

No, I decided not to ask him now. Maybe I would sometime, because I had to know. But not now.

"Almost forgot," Clint said, reeling in his line. "I wanted to show you a couple of moves and holds before we leave. Okay? I learned them way back when I was in the navy, but they're still some of the best."

"Sure," I said.

We carried the poles to shore. Then he stood in front of me and put his hands on my shoulders. "I want you to remember something," he said. "Pins are great, but most matches are won on points. Sure you aim for a pin, but work on the moves and the holds that could get you there. If you don't get the pin, you'll at least get some points. You get what I'm saying?"

I nodded. "Yes."

"Good. Okay. One of the best moves I

learned in the navy was the double leg tackle. Here's the way it's done, so watch and listen closely."

While he showed me the moves, working slowly, he explained them carefully, as if he wanted me to remember them the first time. "Stand in open position," he said, "with your right foot slightly in front of you." He was talking as if he were in my position. "Then shoot your right knee between your opponent's legs, duck your head under his left armpit, and grab his thighs. Then quickly step forward with your left foot, straighten up, lift him, spin on your right knee, and drive him to the mat."

He went on explaining, and I listened as hard as I could. He went over it again and again. Then I took his place and went through the motions, and I realized that it was easier each time.

"You've got it," Clint declared, a pleased tone in his voice. "You've got it, kid. All you need is practice, and you'll be an expert with the double leg."

I promised I'd practice it often. There was at least one guy I was anxious to try it on.

I thanked him, and we shook hands before getting into the car. I hated to leave, because I'd had so much fun, and because I dreaded facing my mother. If she discovered the truth, she'd never trust me again. "You're not only a bum, you're a stinking liar!" she'd cry.

"What're you going to tell your mother?" Clint asked, proving again that he and I were on the same wavelength.

I stared at the street ahead, but saw nothing except the jumbled thoughts in my head. "I . . . I don't know," I said. I was confused, worried. One minute I blamed myself for lying to Mom, the next minute I blamed her for being so down on me.

"Tell her the truth," Clint said. "You'll feel better. She might rake you over the coals, but then again she might not. She might have second thoughts about chewing you out, and realize it's not all your fault. I'd give her that chance if I were you."

His words cleared up the jumble in my head like a fan clears up smoke. "Thanks, Mr. Wagner," I said, feeling relieved. "I was wondering

85

what to do. You're right. I should tell her the truth. And I will."

I thought of the fish. "Will you take the fish?" I asked him. "I hate to think of what she'll say, or do, if she saw . . ."

"I understand." He nodded. "I'll take 'em. There's a family next door to me with four kids. And they all love fish."

"Great," I said.

A few minutes later he stopped in front of the house. I got out, thanked him again, and headed for the kitchen door. When Mom saw me she gave me a look that would've shriveled a shark.

"I saw you get out of that car," she said icily. "Where were you?"

I sat down and, my heart beating like thunder, I told her.

Her face turned cherry red. "You *what?*" she exclaimed. Her voice could've shattered glass. "You went fishing? In spite of my telling you not to?"

I nodded, and calmly explained that I did it because I didn't think I deserved the punishment, that getting into the fight with Max wasn't all my fault, and — maybe the strongest reason of all — that it was probably the only chance I'd ever have of going fishing.

"I'm sorry, Mom," I finished. "I didn't mean to hurt your feelings. But I was hurt, too. I hope you understand."

Gradually, the redness in her cheeks subsided. But her voice remained firm. "Maybe I was a bit harsh with you, and I didn't give you a chance to explain about the fight. But I can't have you sneaking around and disobeying me, either. We'll have to discuss this further when your father comes home. In the meantime, please go up and clean your room."

I nodded obediently and ran up the stairs, only too glad to escape. At least she didn't go completely berserk, I thought with relief. And chances are, if Dad is going to be involved, I'll probably get off with nothing more than a lecture tonight.

Later that afternoon, Carl told Mom that he was going bike riding.

"Can I go with you?" I asked.

"No. I'm going alone," he answered tersely and headed for the door.

I didn't say anything. But right after he left, I went out, too. He had just opened the garage door. We entered the garage, put on our helmets, and got on our bikes.

"I said I'm going alone," Carl said, glaring at me.

"Who said I'm going with you?" I shot back.

I pressed the accelerator, drove past him to the street, and turned left. In the rearview mirror I saw him ride to the street and turn right.

I was hurt and disgusted. I almost followed him to tell him how I felt but I didn't. I just hoped that someday Carl would act like a brother.

I hadn't ridden more than two blocks when I saw a couple of girls skateboarding side by side on the sidewalk. I recognized them immediately: Gail and Barbara.

I pulled up to the curb and cut the engine. "Hi!" I said.

"Oh, look, it's Sean!" Barbara cried, swinging around and stopping in front of me.

"Hi, Sean!" Gail greeted me, skateboarding up to the curb. "Man! What a neat-looking motorcycle! I've never ridden on one before!"

I grinned. "It's not a motorcycle," I said. "It's a dirt bike."

Her eyes sparkled. "Would you give me a ride?"

I was afraid she'd ask me that. "I'm sorry," I said. "I would, but my dad warned me not to give anybody rides."

"Oh, that's okay."

We chatted for about another five minutes, and then more skateboard wheels clacked on the sidewalk. It was the Three Musketeers: the Octopus, the Squasher, and McNeer.

All three of them pulled up sharply in front of us and turned to me. The Octopus glared at me as if I were some kind of insect.

"You get around, don't you, Short Fry?" he snapped. "Gail, you know who you're talking to?"

Her face flushed a little. "Yes, I know to *whom* I'm talking," she answered.

"And you don't care?"

"Why should I care? He's a friend."

"A friend? He's a foe! Do you know he's got my King button and won't give it back to me?"

"I don't care about that, either," she said

90

softly. "Will you leave us alone, please? You interrupted a conversation that doesn't concern you."

Max's face turned rose-red. For a few long seconds there was a heavy silence, then he said, "Let's go, guys. I guess this sister of mine likes little boys."

They whirled as if they were all on a string and scooted down the sidewalk a mile a minute, Max in front.

I turned and stared at Gail.

9

"You're Max's sister?"

She nodded nonchalantly. "Yes. I know what you're thinking and I can't blame you. He can be a pest."

I grinned. "*Can* be?"

"Well, he's mostly like that when he's on the streets with those two goony characters," she said. She took a deep breath and sighed. "I've tried to talk to him about the way he acts at times, but he won't listen."

I wondered if her parents had tried to talk to him, too, but I didn't ask her.

"If you guys don't mind, can we change the subject?" Barbara cut in. "When are you wrestling again?" she asked me.

92

"Thursday night," I said. "Against Gardner."

"Hey!" she exclaimed, smiling broadly. "We're free that night, aren't we? I mean, our guys are wrestling Pierson Friday night."

"Right," Gail said, both of her feet on the skateboard, rocking it back and forth. "Maybe we'll come see you."

"Why not?" Barbara replied.

"That would be nice," I said. But now that I knew Gail was Max's sister, the idea that she would come to see me wrestle didn't especially make me want to do cartwheels. "Ahem . . ." I said, clearing my throat. "Are you sure you want to consort with the enemy?"

"Enemy?" she echoed. "Don't you worry. Max has his friends, I have mine."

I felt better. And I was pretty sure by this time that Barbara hadn't meant to get me in trouble with Max by telling him about the button.

We gabbed for another few minutes, then split up. I rode all the way to the end of the street, then turned left onto the street where Mount Villa Mall was located. I was passing it when some action near the side of the Sears building caught my eye. I slowed down and eased over toward the curb to get a better look.

A guy was standing near the wall with his hands on his hips, watching a wrestling match. But from what I could see, this was no sporting event. Anything went, legal or illegal.

Then I spotted the dirt bike. It was resting against the wall to the guy's left side. A white bike with black trim. The only kid I knew with a bike like that was Carl.

My mind spun. It was the Octopus and his cronies! They were beating up on Carl!

Why him? Then I figured they must be picking on him because they weren't able to get at me earlier. Sure! That was it!

I lifted my bike over the curb, pressed the accelerator lever and felt the bike almost take off from under me. In just a few seconds I was pulling up in front of Nyles and McNeer. They were *both* on top of Carl! Nyles was pinning down his arms and McNeer was sitting on his legs.

I cut the engine, quickly laid the bike down, and dove on Nyles, knocking him off Carl. Then I scrambled to my feet and headed for

McNeer. By now he was pushing himself off of Carl, and shooting puzzled glances from me to Max, as if to ask, "What'll we do now, boss?"

"You jerks!" I yelled. "Leave him alone! Two on one! Great! That's just great!"

"Hey! What's going on?" a man's voice yelled from down in front of Sears.

"A cop!" Max exclaimed. "Let's get out of here!"

He hopped on his skateboard and raced down alongside the building toward the lawn and garden section, Nyles and McNeer at his heels.

The policeman approached Carl and me on a run, gripping his black stick. "Were you guys fighting with that bunch?"

"They were fighting me," Carl explained, brushing dirt off his pantlegs. "I was riding my bike and they stopped me."

"You know them?"

"Yes."

"You want to file charges?"

"No."

"No? You sure? Those punks might want to attack you again, you know."

"I . . . I'll be more careful the next time," Carl promised. I was surprised at his calmness. My own heart was trying to jump out of my chest.

The policeman looked at both Carl and me, his black eyebrows squeezed together above the middle of his stubby nose, as if trying to memorize our faces or recall if he'd seen us before.

"Well, okay," he said finally. "But take my advice. Keep out of trouble, all right?"

We both nodded, and he shook his head and walked away.

"What happened?" I asked Carl. "Why did they jump on you?"

He straightened his helmet and went over to his bike. "Never mind," he said gruffly.

"Never mind?" I echoed.

He got on the bike and started it. From the expression on his face I could tell he wasn't going to talk. But I wanted to know. No matter what he thought of me, I still considered him my brother. And if I could help him, I would. At least, I would try.

I ran over to him and grabbed the handlebars. "Carl! Why did they jump on you?" I repeated.

His eyes met mine, and then he said, "They didn't jump on me, okay? Max wanted me to admit that you've got his King button. I kept saying I didn't know anything about it. Then he started to call you names. Little Punk, Runt, Squirt, names like that."

I kept looking at him, not saying a word.

"I couldn't take it any longer, so I hit him."

"You hit Max?"

He nodded. "Yeah. He hit me once, then had the other two guys jump me."

Carl got into a fight over me? I couldn't believe it!

He started up the engine. But I didn't take my hand off the handlebars. "You started that fight because Max was calling me names?"

"Buzz off," he said.

Anger started to gnaw at my stomach. Carl was still sour on me, no matter what he'd done. Well, who said I needed him to stick up for me, anyway? I could fight my own battles.

"Know what?" I said. "I wish you'd mind

your own business and let me take care of my own."

He glared at me. "Fine with me, brother!" he said. "Now get out of my way!"

He gunned the engine. I let go of the handlebars and he sped up the street, smoke belching from his bike's exhaust. I stared after him, anger still simmering inside me. What a stepbrother, I thought. Will he and I ever become friends? Right now the gap between us seemed ten miles wide.

I sat on my bike, started it up, and wondered what to do next. I didn't feel like going home. All I could do there was sit and mope.

I thought of the school gym. Maybe working out on one of the exercise machines would help relax me.

The gym was a popular place. Over a dozen guys were already there. I changed into my shorts and started lifting barbells. I hadn't been at it more than five minutes when I heard a familiar voice.

"Well, hi, Sean! Building up those biceps to look like Schwarzenegger?"

I paused and grinned at Clint Wagner. From

the sweat glistening on his body, I didn't need two guesses to figure out what he'd been doing.

"Like his brother, anyway," I answered. I didn't even know if Arnold Schwarzenegger had a brother.

I set the barbells down with a heavy sigh. "Had nothing else to do," I said.

"Well, it must have gone well with your mother this morning, or you wouldn't be here."

"Yeah, I told her the truth and she was okay about it." I didn't tell him that the subject wasn't closed yet.

Clint crossed his arms over his chest. "How'd you like to work on some of those holds I showed you?" he asked. "At least it'd be a better use of your time than lifting those barbells."

I shrugged. "Sure."

Why not? I thought. Any coaching I got helped.

Another thing: I kept seeing myself in his face.

10

We got on a mat and worked on the double leg hold and then the single leg until I was sure I had both down pat. Apparently Clint didn't think I had because we went through the practice a couple of more times.

Then he showed me a new hold to use from the stand-up position. "We called this the fishhook tie-up in the navy," he said. "Your aim is to get control of your opponent's shoulders and sink him to his knees. Okay. Watch my moves carefully. I'll go through them a couple of times, then you take my position."

We "attacked." He got his head over my neck and his arms under my armpits, then he hooked his fingers over the top of my shoulders. "Keep your elbows as close as possible to your sides," he said, explaining every move in detail as he went through it. "Then apply pressure upward. See what happens?"

I saw what happened all right. I straightened up as much as I could to try to loosen myself from the hold and to catch my balance. Instantly he let go of me and sprang at my trunk and hips. Before I knew it I was down on the floor.

He grinned as he looked down at me. "Get the picture?" he said, squeezing my arms gently.

I smiled. All the time we'd been wrestling I'd noticed tiny scars on his face. Could they have been caused by fights? A beer bottle, maybe? Was it just a coincidence, I wondered, that both my natural father and Clint Wagner had been in the military? Or was there more to it?

Are you my real dad? I wanted to say. Instead I said, "Yeah, I get it."

He repeated the moves, then had me take over his position. We must have spent forty-five minutes practicing. By then I was tired and thirsty, and Clint was, too. He was breathing

101

harder than I was, but then, he was almost three times my age.

"Time for juice. Right?"

"Right," I said.

We showered and dressed, then went to a nearby coffee shop, where Clint bought us each a glass of orange juice.

I took my time sipping the juice, because I wanted to stay with Clint as long as possible. I wished I could go to his apartment with him. Maybe then I'd have a chance to see pictures of him when he was young. If there was one of him when he was a kid, and he looked like me, there'd be no doubt in my mind that he was my father. Thinking about that possibility sent shivers up my spine.

But he didn't invite me. I figured that he didn't think it would be proper.

It was just as well. By the time we left the coffee shop it was getting close to four o'clock. Mom was probably wondering what had happened to me.

"Thanks for everything, Mr. Wagner," I said. "I sure appreciate your teaching me those holds."

"My pleasure, Sean," he said. "We'll get together again sometime, okay?"

"That'll be great," I said.

"And, look," he added as I headed for my bike, "practice those holds on your brother. Practice them on anybody, but practice them."

"I will," I promised.

Riding homeward I wondered if I could really practice on Carl. The kind of wrestling we did at home seldom involved holds I'd learned from Coach Doran or Coach Collins. It was rough and tumble. We used any kind of a hold that came to us at a particular moment.

But that could change, couldn't it? I thought. I could try a double leg, or a single leg, or a half nelson on him. He wouldn't have to know I was practicing a new hold.

I was home before I realized it. Carl's bike was already in the garage.

I stripped off my gear and went inside. The first person I saw was Carl, chewing on a chocolate chip cookie.

"Where've *you* been?" he asked accusingly.

"At the school gym," I replied.

"What for? More punishment?" He chuckled.

I shrugged. The quickest way to get into a verbal battle with him now would be to tell him the truth, that I'd gone there to get rid of the anger *he* had caused. To avoid that I said, "Right. But Clint Wagner was there, along with some other guys, and he taught me a few holds."

"Oh? Like what?"

"You can find out easily enough if you care to wrestle with me," I answered.

"Sure. Why not?" he said, and took another bite of his cookie. It seemed the air between us was clear again — for the time being, anyway.

Just then Mom appeared at the threshold separating the dining room and kitchen. She scowled at me.

"I'm not exactly pleased about your going out this afternoon, after what happened this morning," she said tersely. "Especially to see Clint Wagner again. I don't think he's a very good influence on you."

Carl looked on, confused but very interested.

"Oh, Mom." Would I ever be able to make

her understand about Clint? He liked me, which was more than I could say about anyone in this house. "I've told you about him. He just wants to teach me some new holds, that's all. What's so terrible about that?"

"Well, all I know is since you've become friends with him you've gotten into more trouble."

I stamped my foot in frustration. "That's crazy, Mom! He's trying to keep me *out* of trouble! When he found out I lied to you this morning, he told me to tell you the truth, and I did."

Carl's eyes grew wider with every word he heard. Finally Mom asked him to leave us alone, and he made his way upstairs . . . very slowly.

Mom sighed. "I just don't know what to do about this."

Why was she making such a big deal out of my seeing Clint? *Maybe it was because she knew more about him than I did. Maybe she knew who he really was, but she didn't want me to find out that he was the man she divorced.*

Well, I wasn't going to let her keep us apart now that I'd found him. "I tell you what, Mom.

As punishment for going against your orders, why don't we say no TV for a week?" I was hoping to impress her with my maturity. And, actually, the fishing trip with Clint had been well worth even worse punishment. But I didn't tell her that.

She rolled her tongue against her cheek as she thought it over. Then she said, "I suppose that's fair. But I don't want you pestering this Clint Wagner person. He's probably a very busy man."

And you wouldn't want the truth to come out, right, Mom? I thought. But I said, "Okay, I won't."

That night I asked Carl if he'd like to wrestle.

"I don't know if I should associate with you," he replied. "You're a troublemaker."

At first I was stunned by his words. Then he flashed that elfish grin of his and said, "Sure, if you're in the mood to lose."

I just smiled.

We put our mats together on the living room floor, stripped to the waist, and went at it. As always, we started from a standing position, just as any dual wrestling match starts.

106

Carl made the first move, grasping my hands, pulling me against him, then swinging his right arm around my neck in a headlock. But this time I twisted out of his hold, ducked my head, and grabbed his legs. I soon had a double leg hold on him and went all the way with it, catching him by surprise.

In seconds I had his shoulders against the mat.

"I think this is called a pin. Don't you?" I said. I couldn't help gloating and silently thanking Clint Wagner for teaching me the moves and the hold.

Carl was speechless, for once. You won't have to fight my battles for me any more, brother, I wanted to tell him. I can fight them myself from now on.

At practice on Monday I learned from Coach Collins that some of the schedules for the upcoming wrestling matches with Gardner Junior High had been changed. The kid I was supposed to wrestle couldn't make it, so my new opponent was a kid named Eddie Lucas.

"He's lighter than you are," Coach Collins

said, "but he hasn't lost a match yet this year. They say he moves like a hummingbird. His nickname is Swifty." He grinned.

"I'll handle him," I said. I was sure I could. Clint had taught me enough good holds to give me a strong advantage, and I had practiced them enough to feel confident about pulling them off.

We did the usual warm-up exercises — motion drills with a partner, push-ups, weight lifting, and so on. Afterwards I asked Coach Collins if I could work out with Bull.

"Mmmmm . . . okay," he finally agreed. "But first, I want to work with you on those two holds we went through last week, the half nelson and the shoulder roll. The half nelson first."

We got into the down position on the mat, and he started the move. In a wink of an eye he had the half nelson on me, and I couldn't budge.

"Let's try it again," he said.

This time I moved quicker and managed to get the hold on *him*. I had a hunch, though, that he hadn't used very much effort to stop me. He wanted to make sure I knew the moves.

We worked on the shoulder rolls a few times. Then, satisfied that I had learned the technique at least, he left to help another couple of guys and let Bull and me go at it.

"Just make sure you don't hurt that guy," the coach said to Bull with a wry grin. "We need him."

"I won't," Bull assured him, and smiled at me.

If you want to discover what wrestling is really like, take on somebody fifty pounds heavier than you are. Most coaches wouldn't permit this one-sided kind of weight match in their schools, and Coach Collins wouldn't have either, if Bull and I hadn't been close friends. But ever since our first match, when we promised not to pull off any crazy stunts that would hurt either of us — me, especially — Coach Collins agreed that our wrestling each other once in a while was okay.

I tried the single leg on Bull first, knowing that trying the double leg would be like trying to grapple Goliath. I got him down and almost twisted him around far enough to get a near fall, but he wiggled himself free — bulled himself free is more like it — and would've pinned me if I hadn't squirmed out of his grasp and jumped to my feet.

We worked on a few other holds together before Coach Collins had us switch with other guys. I was half bushed. If anybody could tire a guy, it was Bull.

Finally Coach Doran blew the whistle. It was 6:30, quitting time.

"Oh, man! About time!" exclaimed Tony, the skinny kid I'd been working out with. He looked as if he'd been drenched with oil. I did, too.

"You can say that again," I said.

We grinned at each other, slapped palms, sighed with relief, and headed for the locker room.

Okay, Eddie Lucas, I thought, I'm ready.

11

When match time came around Thursday evening I wasn't so sure I was ready. There was no wrestling practice on days we had meets, but I felt as if I'd been pulled through a wringer. I blamed it on the restless night I'd had, and a nightmare that was worse than any *Friday the 13th* movie I'd ever seen. A giant octopus grabbed me with its tentacles and brought me toward its wide-open mouth . . .

But I don't want to go into that.

As Coach Collins had said, Eddie Lucas was skinny, but fast. He started off the match with a bang, surprising me with a single leg that ended in a near fall, earning him two points right off the bat.

111

I evened it up with a reversal, but he came back with a half nelson and another near fall. Two more points.

From a stand-up position he tried a double leg on me. But I jumped out of his way, whirled and got an arm around his neck.

"Shoot the half! Shoot the half!" I heard Coach Collins yell.

He was telling me to use the half nelson. But before I could get in position to do so, Lucas twisted out of my hold like a snake for a one-point escape, then tried a single leg on me that drew a whistle from the ref when we both landed off the mat.

From the corner of my eye I saw Clint Wagner standing off to the side in his black-and-white jersey and dark pants. He was eyeing me with concern, as if he wanted to advise me.

Only a father could take such interest in a kid, I thought. *He must be my father. Why don't I ask him? Why doesn't he tell me?*

I wished he *could* advise me. But Coach Collins was doing his best, and so was I. By now I had discovered that Lucas was not only as quick as a hummingbird, he was also tough.

The first period ended. Since Lucas had won the coin-toss at the beginning of the match, he chose the top position to start the second period.

I got down on the mat. Lucas knelt down beside me, grabbed my left arm, and put his right arm across my back. He was in control — so far. I had to pull a surprise on him — a sudden surprise — or the "hummingbird" might roll me in to a near fall, or even a pin. The thought was scary.

The whistle shrilled. I moved the instant I heard it, shot up on my feet, and whirled. At the same time I grabbed something firm, thinking it was Lucas's arm, and I spun in time to see the ref's arm — the one with the red band on it — shoot up. Two fingers jabbed the air.

"Darn!" I said.

I had grabbed Lucas's headgear instead!

The Gardner fans roared. "Way to go, Eddie!" they cried.

The penalty bothered me, but only for a second. Lucas was already on the move, rolling over onto my back, grabbing my left wrist, driving with his legs to power me over onto my

113

back. I could feel his strength and knew that if he succeeded he'd get a near fall for sure. Already he had earned a lot of points and was ahead of me by seven or eight. If he won by eight points — eight to eleven — it would mean a major decision for him and four points for his team. A spread of twelve or more points meant five team points.

I couldn't let that happen. I *wouldn't* let that happen!

Feeling the sweat rolling down my face and into my mouth, I gritted my teeth, gathered all the strength I could, and scored an escape. Then, remembering the double leg tackle that Clint had taught me, I tried it. It worked!

I scored a few more points in the third and last period by reversals and escapes, and when it was over it was *my* hand that the referee raised up.

I'd won by a skimpy margin. But I'd won. I had beaten Swifty, the hummingbird.

I looked up into the stands and saw Mom standing up with other Jefferson Davis fans, smiling and applauding like crazy. Carl wasn't standing, but he was smiling and clapping, too. He may not have been as enthusiastic as Mom, but at least Carl was there. Unlike Dad, who had stayed home again.

I turned and saw Clint looking at me. He smiled, and I smiled back. I hoped he could read the message in my eyes: *Thanks for teaching me some of those holds, Clint. If you hadn't, I wouldn't have won.*

Just then someone called, "Sean!"

I whirled.

"That double leg is a good hold, but I don't remember teaching it to you," Coach Collins said as he came toward me. "You must be doing a lot of homework."

I shrugged and didn't say anything.

"You got away with it this time," he went on, "but you were lucky. It's a clever move, but I don't think you're ready for it. Just stick to the moves I've taught you. Okay?"

He sounded a little perturbed, and I guess he had a right to be. Maybe I'd been listening to Clint more than I should have. Then again, the hold *had* worked . . .

I nodded half-heartedly.

"Congrats, anyway," he said, and walked away.

I was still thinking about what he'd said when a hand grabbed mine and a voice cried in my ear: "Congratulations, Sean! You came through like a champion!"

It was Gail. I looked for her ever-present shadow but didn't see her. Instead, a different girl was with her.

Gail grinned. "You looking for Barbara? She couldn't make it tonight. This is Kate Morris."

"Hi, Kate," I said to the short, chubby girl next to her.

"Hi," she said. Her eyes shifted away from mine, out of shyness, I guessed.

"Thanks for coming," I said to Gail.

But I couldn't help thinking of her as being Max's sister, and just the thought of Max made me sick. In recent weeks no one had gotten me into more trouble than he. Maybe the less I saw of Gail the better.

The overhead lights danced in her eyes. "Well, I admit I was worried for a while. But you came through great."

"Thanks," I said again, turning away. "Sorry. I've got to go."

"So soon?" she exclaimed.

"Yeah," I said over my shoulder.

Just then a trio of guys came up behind Gail and Kate. Speak of the devil! I thought.

"I got to admit you looked okay, Short Fry," Max the Octopus said, one side of his mouth curled in a wry smile. "I can't wait till we get on the mat together. I'll show you some holds that'll make you wish you took up Ping-Pong instead of wrestling."

I matched his cold stare. "I can't wait, either," I said.

"Max! You're a jerk, you know that?" Gail said irritably. "You don't care *what* you say! You don't care about anyone else's feelings! I think you're . . . despicable!" Her small fists were clenched. She was furious enough to belt him.

So was I. But her reaction didn't exactly please me, either.

It seemed like *everybody* was trying to fight my battles for me. And I didn't like it one bit.

12

When we got home the front door was locked. But there was a light on in the living room, so we were sure Dad was there.

Mom knocked and he opened the door for us. He was in shirtsleeves and wearing his reading glasses.

"Well," he said, studying us, "from your pleased expressions I don't need to ask you who won. But to make sure, I will, anyway. Who won?"

"Sean did, of course," Mom said elatedly, removing her coat and handing it over to him. "You missed a good match, Troy. It was nip and tuck most of the time."

"Mostly nip," Carl chipped in.

"Sorry," Dad said, shaking his head. "I guess I'm a poor fan. But you know how I feel about wrestling. It just doesn't . . ." He shrugged, searching for a reason.

"That's okay, Dad," I said. "A lot of guys don't care for wrestling. Our principal, Mr. McClure, doesn't. He's never been to a wrestling meet. But he admits it's a good sport. Good, clean exercise, he calls it."

"That I can admit, too," Dad said, nodding.

Just the same, I wished Dad had been at the meet. I was proud of the win. It was a nip and tucker, all right. It would've been nice to have seen him up there in the stands cheering for me.

But maybe his not being my natural father had something to do with it. If he were, he probably would've been there, whether he cared for wrestling or not. A lot of other fathers came, and I bet they weren't all wrestling nuts, either. They came because their sons were there, giving it their best, putting every bit of their heart in it, in a one-on-one competition.

Then I thought of Clint Wagner, of the pleased, proud expression on his face after my match with Lucas was over. Only a father could look that way. *Oh, Clint! Please tell me you're my father! Please!*

The next evening — Friday — after I returned home from wrestling practice, I waited for a call from Clint. I was hoping he'd ask me to go fishing with him again. Maybe this time I'd finally break the ice. Maybe I'd have the nerve to ask him: *Clint, are you my father?*

But eight o'clock came and he didn't call. And then eight-thirty, and nine o'clock rolled by, and he still didn't call.

I was disappointed. Well, maybe he had a commitment. Or maybe a date. *Would he still date women at his age?* Maybe. There were a lot of *maybes* when it came to Clint.

Thinking about Clint kept me awake half of the night. I could call him in the morning, I thought. Or I could ride over to his place. I didn't know where he lived, but I could find out by looking it up in the phone book. Mom

wouldn't have to know about it — she'd think I was pestering him. But what was so terrible about visiting a friend, anyway?

After breakfast the next morning I checked out Clint's address in the phone directory and rode over there on my bike. Mom was busy vacuuming the rugs, so she wouldn't even miss me.

When I rode up toward the apartment building where he lived, I saw a small U-Haul truck parked in front of the main entrance, its tailgate down.

I pulled up beside it, letting the engine of the bike idle, and wondered if somebody was moving in or out. I didn't have long to wonder.

Within five seconds the entrance door swung open and a guy wearing jeans, a sweatshirt, and a baseball hat came out, carrying a large cardboard box.

"Mr. Wagner!" I said, stunned. "What . . . what are you doing?"

"Oh, hi, Sean," he said. He placed the box in the truck and looked at me. Sweat shone on his forehead. "I'm moving."

"Moving?" Oh, no! My mind whirled.

"Yes, I'm moving, Sean," he said softly. "I would've called you, don't worry."

"Why? Where?" I stammered.

"I got a new job, and it's out of town," he explained. "I hadn't planned on staying here forever, anyway. When there was a job opening here, I applied for it and got it. But it wasn't one I hoped to spend the rest of my life doing. It was just to fill the gap until I found the right one, the one I wanted. And that's what happened."

"You mean you didn't come to Mount Villa just to . . . just to referee?" I asked, feeling a lump form in my throat. *You didn't come to be near me, your son?* was what I really wanted to ask him.

He smiled. "Oh, no. I can referee anywhere, and I have. I'll probably get a refereeing job in my new town, too. A head refereeing job, if possible, since my other job will be permanent."

Clint took f his cap and mopped his brow. "Well, I've got to get a move on. I have to be out of here by tonight."

I should've offered to help, but my tongue — like the rest of my body — seemed frozen in place. He was leaving, just like that. I'd probably never see him again. And that meant I'd been wrong about him all along.

Clint must have read the disappointment in my face. "It's too bad this had to happen just when we were becoming friends. But pretty soon you'll be too busy for an old guy like me, with girlfriends and wrestling and all. Just remember some of those new moves and holds I taught you, okay?"

He extended his hand and, after a moment, I shook it.

"Sure," I managed to mutter. "Thanks for everything."

Suddenly my body was in working order again, and I pulled out of the driveway without looking back. I rode off down the street, thoughts churning in my head. Who needed him, anyway? I'd gotten along fine before I met him. I didn't need Clint or anyone else.

I must have headed for home out of habit, because I found myself there in a matter of

minutes. But Carl was polishing up his bike in the driveway, and I was in no mood to deal with him.

Instead, I gunned the motor and turned around. I needed to be alone, to clear my head. I knew just where to go — the dirt bike track.

I hadn't ridden more than a block when I heard a motor behind me and, glancing at my rearview mirror, I saw that it was Carl. Was he following me? I wondered. Well, if he was, I wasn't going to pay any attention to him.

I reached the track — there was no gate — and started to ride around it. Carl was still some fifty feet behind me. Figuring on widening the gap between us, I accelerated and felt the bike take off like a rocket. The track was bumpier than I'd remembered, but it had been three or four months since I'd ridden on it. I laughed out loud as the bike bounced crazily on the rough track. I went faster and faster, enjoying the rush of air against my face and the roar of the engine underneath me.

For a second I glanced at the rearview mirror and saw Carl far behind me. He had one hand

off the handlebars, signaling me hard to slow down.

I laughed. "Slow down yourself, brother!" I shouted into the wind.

I'd barely gotten "brother" out when the front wheel of my bike struck a sharp bump and the bike swerved. Icy terror shot up my spine as I lost my grip on the handlebars. The bike reeled over onto its side, and I went with it.

13

Carl pulled up beside me. "You okay?"

I nodded as I slowly got to my feet. I was bruised and dirty, but nothing was broken.

"Why'd you follow me, anyway?" I snapped at Carl. Now Mom would find out, and I'd be in hot water again.

"I don't know," Carl said. "I felt like it. And you looked —"

I cut him off. "Well, why don't you bug off? I've got everything under control."

"Could've fooled me," Carl muttered before taking off.

After he left, I lifted my bike and checked it for damage. Other than a few scratches here and there it looked okay. The engine started up again the first time I tried it.

What a relief. The last thing I wanted to do was ask Dad to repair any damages.

But, as Yogi Berra said, it's not over til it's over, and I still had to face Mom.

When I got home, it was obvious that Carl hadn't squealed to her, but my dirt-smudged clothes said enough. At first she thought I'd been in another fight, and to set her straight I had to tell her the truth.

Her face turned beet red, and for a minute I thought she was going to swat me. But she didn't. She just lit into me with words. "I don't know what to do with you, Sean. I really don't. Then again maybe I do. Whether it'll do any good I don't know, but you're grounded for the rest of the weekend. Is that clear?"

It was clear enough. But it was a punishment I didn't think I deserved. No one had gotten hurt, after all.

Trying to hide my resentment, I went upstairs to shower, change into clean clothes, and hole up in my room.

When noontime came I was still there, lying on my bed.

"Sean! You gonna have lunch?" I heard Carl call to me.

"No!" I shouted back.

I was hungry, but I wasn't going to eat. The heck with it, I thought. The heck with everybody. Nobody around here cared about me, let alone loved me. Now that the only guy in the world who had ever shown any interest in me was leaving, I might as well be dead.

Sometime later I heard a car start up and back out of the driveway. I went to the window and peeked out. It was Mom, driving away alone. Maybe she was going out to shop or visit a friend.

Two minutes later Carl went out and rode away on his dirt bike.

I could hear the television on in the living room. Dad was probably watching a football game.

I stood there a minute, thinking. What right did Mom have to keep me cooped up? I was fourteen, not a little kid.

The more I thought about it, the angrier I

got. I decided I wasn't going to stay here another minute. I was going out.

I put on my boots, jacket, and helmet and left my room, closing the door behind me as quietly as possible. I didn't want Dad to hear me, even though I figured he couldn't care less whether I left or not.

I treaded quietly through the hall, as the excited voice of the announcer on TV described an intercepted pass. I sneaked out of the kitchen, entered the opened garage, and got on my bike.

I was wheeling it out of the garage when someone stepped in front of me. It was Dad. I froze.

"So, you're disobeying your mother again," he said calmly. If it was Mom, she would've grabbed me and yanked me off the bike, but Dad never showed any emotion.

I sucked in a deep breath. "I don't think she's being fair."

"But she's your mother," he said. "Whether it's fair or not, you're expected to obey her."

"I'm no little kid!"

"Then why are you behaving like one?"

"I'm not!"

"But you are, Sean," he said. "You're fourteen, and acting like ten. You think you can do anything you want and get away with it. Well, you're wrong. We're your parents, and we decide what's best for you."

"But how can you decide that when you don't even know me?" I blurted out.

A look of pain crossed his face, and I immediately regretted my words.

"Maybe we don't know you," Dad replied after a minute. "But maybe that's because you haven't been acting like yourself lately. Did you ever think about that?"

I shrugged. I didn't know what I thought anymore. I was tired of thinking.

I started to back up the bike.

"That's right," Dad said. "Put it back. Don't let your mother get any angrier than she already is. Show her that much respect, at least."

I put my bike back into place. Then I walked out of the garage. As I passed Dad, he grabbed my arm.

"Thanks, Sean," he said.

I just nodded and went back into the house.

I didn't feel much better. I was still mad at Mom, but I wasn't up to creating any more waves.

I had another problem to face later that week: we were meeting Franklin on Friday, and I was scheduled to wrestle my old nemesis, Max "the Octopus" Rundel.

At a practice meet on Tuesday with Bosworth Junior High, I was matched up with a dark-haired kid named Tommy Burke. He was about two inches taller than me and about two pounds heavier. This would be my last chance to try out my holds and moves before tangling with the Octopus. I was hot and eager. I was going to beat Tommy Burke no matter what it took.

Burke seemed quite slow, or maybe too cautious, and I earned the first few points on a half nelson. Seconds later Burke got a quarter nelson on me and started to work it into a headlock — legally, the way he was applying it — making me realize that my first impression of him had been wrong. This kid knew what he was doing.

I didn't pick up another point during the first period. He picked up five.

"More halves, Sean," Coach Collins said softly to me as Burke and I got in position for the second period. "And the roll."

He was referring to the half nelson and the shoulder roll. But I figured I understood Burke better than he did. He wasn't wrestling Burke, I was. I knew the effective moves.

I considered using the double leg, one of Clint's favorite holds. But just thinking of Clint hurt. I wanted to forget about him and everything he'd taught me. I didn't need his help, either.

I tried my own version of a leg hold, but it didn't work, and Burke scored a reversal. Little by little he kept earning points — a lot more than I was. Not only was I getting beat, I was getting angry.

In the third period I tried every hold I could think of on him, including a half nelson that I wanted to turn into a pin. I figured it was the only way to stop him now.

The ref declared the hold illegal. More points for Burke.

I was furious.

By the time the match ended, Burke was so

far ahead of me I didn't even want to know the score. I left the mat in a huff.

"Sean!" Coach Collins yelled at me. "You didn't listen to a word I said!"

"I'm sorry, Coach," I said numbly, sweat rolling down my face and into my eyes.

"That wasn't like you, Sean," he went on. "You used any move that came into your head, except the ones I taught you, and it showed."

"I suppose I did," I said, and I started to head for the locker room, leaving him staring at my back. I was in no mood to discuss the match any further.

"Sean!"

I paused. Gail's voice.

I looked behind me. Barbara was with her. "Hi," I said.

They were both staring at me as if I'd changed into a werewolf.

"We came to see you wrestle tonight," Gail said softly. "But that didn't look like you on the mat."

"Oh? Who did I look like?"

"Those guys on TV," she answered. "Those

big, he-men wrestlers who put on a show, not like the Sean Bailor I've seen."

Her words stung like a bee. I tried to think of something to say in return, but my mind went blank.

She wasn't finished. "I thought you were smarter than my brother, that you were a real athlete. But I guess I was mistaken." She turned and stalked off toward the exit door with Barbara at her heels.

I stood glued to the floor, staring at the closed door, pondering Gail's words.

I guess I hadn't been too far off when I thought I must have looked like a werewolf to her.

Carl and I rode home with Bull and his parents. Because it was just a practice meet, Mom hadn't come. I wondered what she would've said about my performance. Nothing good, that's for sure. Carl's remark was enough to make up for hers.

"I hate to think of what Max is going to do to you on Friday," he said. "If I were you, I'd forfeit."

14

"The half, Sean! The half!"

"The double leg, Sean!"

"Pin 'im, Max!"

The cries came from both the Jefferson Davis and Franklin fans, like armchair coaches watching a Saturday afternoon football game. I ignored them, just as Max did, I'm sure. We were fighting our battle now, the battle we'd been talking about ever since we'd gotten into our first scrap.

The match with Burke was behind me. This was a new one, the big one, and with an opponent who had brought me nothing but trouble: Max "the Octopus" Rundel. He still thought he was king, and I had to knock off that crown . . . forever.

Right now he had me in a near cradle, a hold he was leading up to when he swished his right arm over the back of my neck and started to reach his left through my crotch. He was grunting as he exerted all the pressure he could to put me away.

"Shoot the half, Sean! The half!"

Coach Collins's voice came to me as I was on my hands, my left knee down on the mat, and I made my move. I rolled over onto my back and swung my right arm around his neck. In a second I had him in a prone position, got my arm under his near shoulder and twisted him toward the floor to apply the half nelson.

"That a way! You've got him, Sean! You've got him!" I heard the coach cry.

I was using all the muscle and power I had to finish the Octopus off — and the match had started only a minute ago. Already he'd won several points — on reversals and escapes. Me, I had only two, both on escapes.

I couldn't complete the half nelson. Max's sweaty body slithered out of my grasp, and, like a puppet yanked up by a string, he was on his feet, hands held out to defend himself.

Another escape for him. Another point. The points were building up, slowly, surely.

He was panting, just as I was. Our eyes locked as we tried to read each other's mind. What was he going to do next? I'd heard that the single leg was his best move. But he had already tried it on me and failed. Twice. Did he have another favorite?

But I couldn't wait for him to think of his next move. I had to make mine . . . *now*.

I thought of the double leg, the hold Clint had taught me. Could I count on it? Could I count on anything Clint had told me? He'd left me in the lurch.

The few seconds I hesitated allowed Max to get a single leg on me. Luckily, by sheer strength and quickness, I was able to squirm out of it and earn a reversal.

"The double leg, Sean!" I heard a voice shout.

At first I thought I was imagining Clint's voice. But no, it was Carl's. He echoed my own hunch that it would work. *Why not use everything*

I knew? Clint had only wanted me to win; what was the harm in following his advice? I was still the one who had to make the moves!

Fired up with new hope and determination, I dove at Max's legs and grabbed him above the knees. The Octopus let out a grunt and fell backward, putting both his arms around my shoulders as he did so, and spreading his legs to avoid my completing the hold.

His effort worked. I was able to get a strong hold of only one leg, but I used it to the best advantage. I rose quickly to my feet, lifting his leg up off the mat with the hope of dumping him and then falling on him with maybe a double leg, a half nelson, or even — oh, wow — a treetop finish, in which I would have him up on one leg, dump him, and shoot for the pin.

I got as far as pulling the Octopus's leg up to my right ear when the whistle blew, ending the first period. I'd never know whether I would have pinned him then or not.

Every second that we'd been together on the mat I'd learned more and more about the Octopus. My final analysis was he was just as tough as, or tougher than, he had pretended to be.

The Octopus had his choice of position when the second period started, and he chose to be on top. The wrestler in the top position has a definite advantage. If the guy on top is smart — smart, strong, and aggressive — the guy below might as well kiss the match good-bye.

I thought back to what Gail had said. I *was* smarter than Max — usually. Now I just had to make myself as strong and aggressive as he was. That was the only way I would be able to stop him from taking me.

We assumed our positions, the ref blew his whistle, and I moved. The Octopus moved at the same time, yanking my arm back to force me to fall flat on my noggin. But I rolled with the move instead and slipped out of his control.

Simultaneously a cheer exploded from the Jefferson Davis fans.

I was hoping for at least a few seconds' rest, when the Octopus dove at me, catching me by surprise. In a moment he had a half nelson on me and was pushing my shoulders against the mat.

Oh, God! I thought. No! I couldn't let him pin me! I couldn't let him win!

I could see his sweat-glistening face inches above mine, his dark, fiery eyes glaring like an angry tiger's, his white teeth fanned out like a picket fence.

"This is it, Small Fry!" he whispered. "This . . . is . . . it!"

In that brief moment, when he lessened his concentration — and loosened his hold just a bit — I jerked up my right hip, broke out of his control, and rolled up into a sitting position. At the same time I grabbed the arm that he had wrapped around me, pulled it tight against my stomach and rolled over, dragging him after me. Another roar came from the stands — from the Franklin fans for the Octopus's getting a near fall, and from the Jefferson Davis fans for my earning an escape and then a takedown.

But Max twisted his wrist free from my grasp and in a lightning-fast move got behind me, wrapping his left arm over my left shoulder and his right around my stomach. The Franklin fans cheered again as the ref's right arm — the arm with the green band — went up and two fingers flashed.

The Octopus was rolling up more points, and I said a silent "thank you" prayer as the whistle blew, ending the second period.

I took the top position as the third period started, one arm wrapped around the Octopus's right shoulder, the other gripping his left arm. I thought of the chicken wing, a hold Coach Collins had taught me. But you had to be careful with it, he had warned me, or you could get points scored against you, or even injure your opponent.

Was it worth it? I thought. Should I take the risk?

I considered Max's build, his strength. It would take a lot to hurt him. And he was already far ahead of me in points. How much, I didn't know. He had to be at least eight points ahead, which meant a major decision and four points for his team. He was well on the way to what the newspapers would call "an undisputed victory."

What did I have to lose?

I'll use it, I decided.

The whistle blew. I moved, tightening my grip on his right shoulder and dropping my hand to grab his left arm. At the same time, he rolled hard over onto his side, pulling me with him, and in seconds had me in a half nelson.

Oh, no! my mind screamed as I heard the Franklin fans cheer. The Octopus was heading for a superior.

Seconds ticked on as I thought of holds both Clint and Coach Collins had taught me. I had little chance of winning now. No chance at all, except by a pin.

Max was shooting for a fall himself when, suddenly, I was in position to put the leg trap on him. I earned a point for the escape, then two more for a takedown. Dead tired, I saw that we both were near the edge of the mat, and that the Octopus, sweating profusely, his chest heaving with each breath, was deliberately crawling off of it.

The whistle shrilled. We rose to our feet and stood in the center of the mat. Quickly I dug back into my think tank for a hold I could put on the Octopus to finish him. I was probably out of my mind. Hoping to finish him was like hoping to win a million-dollar lottery.

But I couldn't let him win. He'd never let me

forget it. And he'd made my life miserable enough already.

I stood with my right foot slightly in front of me, clearly remembering Clint's instructions for a move and hold I felt was now my only hope.

The whistle shrilled again. This time I moved before the Octopus did. I shot my right knee between his legs, ducked my head under his left armpit, and grabbed his thighs. I was tired and breathing heavily. But Max was bushed, too. That's where I had a slight advantage: he may have been taller than me, and stronger, but I had more stamina.

I stepped forward, straightened up, lifted him off the mat, spun, and drove him to the mat. I pounced on top of him as I did so, got a half nelson on him, and started to press his shoulders to the mat.

I was close to pinning him! Press harder! Harder! I told myself. I was sure that this was it, and even more sure when the shouts and screams of the Franklin Junior High fans threatened to bring down the ceiling.

But it wasn't over yet. The Octopus uttered

a loud grunt, and his right hip sprang up, breaking my hold.

But, quick as he was, I was quicker. I yanked him back down on the mat, this time exerting all the strength I could muster to press his shoulders against it. His face showed that he was straining every muscle in his body.

And out of the corner of my eyes I saw the ref get down on his belly next to us, raise his right hand . . .

And then bring it down . . . once . . . twice . . .

I leaped to my feet, my ears filled with the cries, the cheers, the whistles of the Jefferson Davis fans.

I had won! I had pinned the mighty Octopus!

A hand grabbed my right wrist and lifted it up high. "The winner!" the ref announced.

The Jefferson Davis fans came running down the stands then, yelling like crazy. They hugged me and shook my hands. Mom was teary eyed as she threw her arms around me. Carl was beaming.

"You did it, bro," he declared, smiling broadly. "You beat the Octopus."

I'd never seen him so delighted about my winning in my life.

And there was Dad! I stared in disbelief, a lump forming in my throat. He hadn't ridden to the meet with the rest of us. He'd probably decided to come at the last minute. I didn't care. He was there.

He grabbed my shoulders and pulled me against him. "Good work, son!" he said. "Darn good work!"

"Thanks, Dad!" I whispered, my tear-stained eyes closed.

When I opened them again I saw another face, not more than a foot away.

"Congratulations, Sean," Gail said softly. "You were terrific."

"Thanks," I said.

She waved and walked away. I wondered if I'd see her again, if I'd ever get a chance to talk to her again. Well, there'd be plenty of other meets between her school and mine . . . who knew?

A hand tapped my shoulder. I turned. It was Max.

"Congrats, Bailor," he said. "I hate to say this,

but you're a better man than I thought you were."

"Thanks, Max," I replied. "You're pretty good yourself." Then I remembered something. "Wait here," I said, and ran to the locker room. A few seconds later I was back.

"Here," I said, holding out his I AM KING button. "This belongs to you."

He looked at it, then at me. "Keep it," he said. "You deserve it more than I do."

"But it's yours," I declared. "And I don't want it. Please take it."

Reluctantly, he took it. Then, after gazing at it for a moment, he crushed it in his hand, turned, and left.

Watching him walk away, I knew that tonight's defeat had earned me more than points. I knew the Octopus and his cronies would never torment me again.

Mom grabbed my hand and gently squeezed it. "Take your shower, Sean," she said. "And then we'll go home for a real family celebration. How'd you like that?"

"I'd like that a lot, Mom," I said with a grin. "More than you know."

How many of these Matt Christopher sports classics have you read?

Baseball

❑ Baseball Pals
❑ Catcher with a Glass Arm
❑ Challenge at Second Base
❑ The Diamond Champs
❑ The Fox Steals Home
❑ Hard Drive to Short
❑ The Kid Who Only
   Hit Homers
❑ Look Who's Playing
   First Base
❑ Miracle at the Plate
❑ No Arm in Left Field
❑ Shortstop from Tokyo
❑ The Submarine Pitch
❑ Too Hot to Handle
❑ The Year Mom Won
   the Pennant

Basketball

❑ The Basket Counts
❑ Johnny Long Legs
❑ Long Shot for Paul
❑ Red-Hot Hightops

Dirt Bike Racing

❑ Dirt Bike Racer
❑ Dirt Bike Runaway

Football

❑ Catch That Pass!
❑ The Counterfeit Tackle
❑ Football Fugitive
❑ The Great Quarterback
   Switch
❑ Tight End
❑ Touchdown for Tommy
❑ Tough to Tackle

Ice Hockey

❑ Face-Off
❑ The Hockey Machine
❑ Ice Magic

Soccer

❑ Soccer Halfback

Track

❑ Run, Billy, Run

All available in paperback from Little, Brown and Company

Join the Matt Christopher Fan Club!

To become an official member of the Matt Christopher Fan Club,
send a self-addressed, stamped envelope (10 x 13, 3 oz. of postage) to:

Matt Christopher Fan Club
34 Beacon Street
Boston, MA 02108